Proposals for Government Credit Allocation

Leland B. Yeager
With a foreword by Yale Brozen

American Enterprise Institute for Public Policy Research
Washington, D.C.

Leland B. Yeager is Paul Goodloe McIntire professor of economics at the University of Virginia.

Library of Congress Cataloging in Publication Data

Yeager, Leland B
 Proposals for government credit allocation.

 (AEI studies ; 181)
 Includes bibliographical references.
 1. Credit control—United States. I. Title. II. Series: American Enterprise Institute for Public Policy Research. AEI studies ; 181.
 HG3729.U5Y4   332.7   77-15776
 ISBN 0-8447-3281-8

AEI Studies 181

Printed in the United States of America

CONTENTS

FOREWORD *Yale Brozen*   1

1 PROPOSALS AND ARGUMENTS   5

Precedents   6
Weapons of Selective Credit Control   12
Arguments for Controls and Their Weaknesses   14
Imperfections, Existing Controls, and
    Differential Impacts   25

2 LOOPHOLES AND THEIR CONSEQUENCES   31

Fungibility   32
Circumvention through the Market   35
The Costs of Circumvention   39
Loopholes and the Proliferation of Controls   42
Further Costs   46
Experience Abroad   50

3 WHAT KIND OF ECONOMIC SYSTEM?   61

Ultimate Consequences   61
Alternatives   62
Where to Apply Corrective Measures   63
Should the Government Guide the
    Pattern of Economic Activity?   65
Why Is the Idea So Durable?   70
An Appraisal in Context   74

FOREWORD

Proposals for government credit allocation are coming with increasing frequency. In part, this is a consequence of the unprecedented string of federal deficits draining capital from other uses. Equally important has been the proliferation of government programs in the past assisting some borrowers in obtaining funds by guaranteeing or subsidizing loans to them. Since 1960, federal borrowing and federally assisted borrowing have absorbed an increasing proportion of total credit, rising from 13 percent of the total to 36 percent.[1] This has decreased the funds available to other borrowers, forced up the interest rates they must pay to obtain funds, and led to their demands for government assistance. Thus, credit-allocation programs beget more such programs.

Credit-control programs also proliferate, as Professor Yeager points out in this study, because the fungibility of funds and the diversity of financial channels make it easy to circumvent the "negative" controls placed on any one channel. The loopholes lead authorities to erect additional controls on one channel after another, proliferating controls in their chase of the will-o'-the-wisp of omniscient and omnipresent guidance of the use of capital. In the government's attempt to control the flow of capital, negative controls on what financial institutions are allowed to do are supplemented with "positive" controls such as government guarantees and subsidies for favored borrowers.

That the federal government has already come to play an overwhelming role in providing access to the available supply of capital

---

[1] Murray L. Weidenbaum and Reno Harnish, *Government Credit Subsidies for Energy Development* (Washington, D.C.: American Enterprise Institute for Public Policy Research, 1976), p. 14, Table 1.

1

Table 1
MAJOR FEDERAL CREDIT PROGRAMS, FISCAL YEAR 1975
(new commitments, in millions of dollars)

Category and Agency	Direct Loans		Guaranteed Loans	Government Sponsored Enterprises	Total
	On budget	Off budget			
Aid to Business					
Commerce	$15	—	$699	—	$714
Interior	22	—	—	—	22
Transportation	37	—	177	—	214
Export-Import Bank	—	$3,813	8,708	—	12,521
Federal Deposit Insurance Corporation	100	—	1,723	—	1,823
General Services Administration	—	—	72	—	72
Small Business Administration	520	—	1,365	—	1,885
U.S. Railway Association	—	34	—	—	34
Subtotal	694	3,847	12,744	—	17,285
Aid to Farmers					
Agriculture	6,329	1,060	8,577	—	15,966
Farm credit agencies	—	—	—	$20,910	20,910
Subtotal	6,329	1,060	8,577	20,910	36,876
Aid to Local Governments					
Housing and Urban Development	590	—	1,252	—	1,842
Justice	40	—	—	—	40
District of Columbia	232	—	—	—	232
Subtotal	862	—	1,252	—	2,114
Aid to Individuals					
Health, Education, and Welfare	543	—	1,388	—	1,931
Housing and Urban Development	11,779	—	4,791[a]	—	16,570
Veterans Administration	524	—	3,602[a]	—	4,126
Federal Home Loan Bank System	1,305	—	—	12,694	13,999
Federal National Mortgage Association	—	—	—	4,434	4,434
Student Loan Marketing Association	—	—	—	144	144
Subtotal	14,151	—	9,781	17,272	41,204
Aid to Foreign Governments					
Security assistance	437	—	616	—	1,053
Development assistance	478	—	26	—	504
Subtotal	915	—	642	—	1,557
Miscellaneous					
Federal Financing Bank[a]	—	—	—	—	—
All other	95	—	6	—	101
Subtotal	95	—	6	—	101
GRAND TOTAL	23,046	4,907	33,002	38,182	99,137

[a] Duplicate transactions have been eliminated.
Source: Compiled from *Special Analyses, Budget of the United States Govern-*

is made obvious by a glance at Table 1. Although only program categories in which positive controls are used are displayed (none of the negative programs are shown), we can see that nearly $100 billion of the available supply of capital is allocated by the political process under this one set of controls. It is no wonder that less-favored borrowers are ever more loudly bewailing the shortage of capital.

The proliferation of credit controls occurs not only to plug loopholes and to satisfy those deprived by absorption of capital by those politically favored previously but also because of the effect of subsidized programs on the use of our resources. For example, the Rural Electrification Program provides subsidized capital for the construction of small-scale, fuel-inefficient generating plants. As concern for the future availability of energy grows, we hear proposals for the subsidized provision of capital for the development of new energy sources. It would seem wiser to stop subsidizing fuel-inefficient means of supplying electric power and the use of electric power, but a political constituency has been developed which prevents the political process from working in this way. Instead, another credit-allocation program is proposed to offset the first, and thus further proliferation occurs.

Still another cause of excessive controls is the failure of one set of controls to accomplish their objective, leading authorities to try additional programs. As Professor Yeager points out, for example, the various special programs for providing or subsidizing mortgage credit have apparently not increased the stock of housing, although that was their intended purpose. It has merely increased the amount of mortgages on residential property, since the controls used to funnel capital into mortgages make this a cheaper source of finance than those that would normally be used. The resulting frustration has led to the proposal of additional credit-control programs.

As credit-allocating programs continue to grow, an increasing portion of our capital is divided among various uses according to the political clout that can be exercised on behalf of each. Whom you know and with whom you have influence becomes more important in obtaining capital than how productively you can use it. Capital is diverted from more productive uses to politically determined applications. The possibilities for corruption and tyranny

ment, Fiscal Year 1977. Murray L. Weidenbaum, "An Economic Analysis of the Federal Government's Credit Programs," Working Paper No. 18 (St. Louis: Center for the Study of American Business, Washington University, January 1977).

multiply, and the national income pie shrinks as a consequence of this process. The national income pie shrinks as an increasing proportion of our capital is allocated by the political process—not only because of its diversion from more productive uses but also because more and more of our resources are devoted to winning political influence, as that becomes the road to access to available capital and subsidies.

The cost of controls is turning out to be more than just the cost of administration, enforcement, and compliance, of inefficiencies resulting from avoidance and of allocation of capital to less productive uses, and obsolescence of knowledge. As Professor Yeager shows, the moral foundations of law are being eroded, and the very nature of our economic system is changing. The price of controls is becoming our freedom and our democracy. The Gulliver of America is becoming ensnared and bound by the twine of the Lilliputians. Our citizenry is losing control of its government and is more and more being controlled by it.

YALE BROZEN
Graduate School of Business
University of Chicago

4

1

PROPOSALS AND ARGUMENTS

From time to time the idea revives of using government agencies to guide the allocation of credit to "worthy" borrowers or purposes. The notion gains popularity when credit tightens and such borrowers find loans harder to get or interest rates higher than they would like. Frequently the government itself contributes to this state of affairs as it competes with other borrowers for funds to cover its budget deficits—a phenomenon which has come to be called "crowding out."[1] But those who want to use governmental powers to allocate credit in this way seldom suggest that the drains of capital could be reduced by reducing governmental deficits. Instead, they usually propose to meet the problem they perceive with another credit-allocation program.

The proposals for government credit allocation do not stand alone. They reflect a widespread, if tacit, attitude about government's role in people's business and personal affairs. It would be narrow and incomplete to appraise each particular proposal for government intervention alone, on its own supposed merits, without concern for how the *combination* of proposed measures might alter the country's economic and political system. Credit-control proposals will be considered in this broad context, but only after examination of some specific aspects of credit controls.[2]

---

[1] Roger W. Spencer and William P. Yohe, "The 'Crowding-Out' of Private Expenditures by Fiscal Policy Actions," Federal Reserve Bank of St. Louis *Review*, vol. 52, no. 10 (October 1970), pp. 12-24, and Karl Brunner and Allan H. Meltzer, "Government, the Private Sector, and 'Crowding Out,'" *The Banker*, July 1976, pp. 765-69.

[2] Instead of pretending to originality, this study distills the key points scattered throughout a rather unsatisfactory literature, adding some reflections. Thoroughly argued proposals for selective credit controls are few or non-

Precedents

Many measures intended to affect credit allocation have already been tried in the United States, though not in a coordinated way. "Negative" measures restrict certain loans. The Federal Reserve limits loans to carry corporation stocks to a specified percentage of the value of the stock pledged as collateral. During World War II, in 1948–1949, and during the Korean War, the Federal Reserve had authority to specify minimum down payments and maximum maturities for consumer and real estate loans. The Interest Equalization Tax and the Foreign Credit Restraint Program of the 1960s and early 1970s sought to restrain purchases of foreign securities and other loans to foreign borrowers.

"Positive" measures favor particular types of credit. Tax benefits to home-mortgage debtors and personal borrowers in general are well known, as is the exemption from federal income tax of interest earned on bonds of state and local governments. During the 1930s the government experimented on a small scale with promoting credit for repair and modernization of houses and for purchase of electrical appliances.[3] It has made and continues to make low-cost (subsidized) loans to rural electric and telephone cooperatives.[4] The Export-Import Bank provides export credit. The Federal Land Banks, Intermediate Credit Banks, and Banks for Cooperatives promote credit to agriculture. The government has subsidized or guaranteed loans to veterans and to students. The Veterans Administration and the Federal Housing Administration guarantee mortgage loans. The Federal Home Loan Banks float bonds and relend the proceeds to savings and loan associations, which in turn invest mostly in mortgages. The Federal National Mortgage Association (originally a government enterprise), the Government National Mortgage Association, the Public Housing Administration, and the Farmers Home Administration also promote credit for housing; so, in earlier years, did the Reconstruction Finance Corporation, the Homeowners Loan Corporation, and the Federal Farm Mortgage Corporation. By late 1976, "federal and

---

existent, which leaves writers who would examine the proposed measures wrestling with ghosts.

[3] Paul F. Smith, "A Review of the Theoretical and Administrative History of Consumer Credit Controls," in *Studies in Selective Credit Policies*, ed. Ira Kaminow and James M. O'Brien (Philadelphia: Federal Reserve Bank of Philadelphia, 1975), pp. 135-37.

[4] Lester V. Chandler, *The Economics of Money and Banking*, 6th ed. (New York: Harper & Row, 1973), p. 263.

related agencies" held 13 percent of the mortgage debt outstanding in the United States.[5]

Testifying in February 1975, Treasury Secretary William Simon said that some 150 federal credit-assistance programs were already channeling about $50 billion a year into uses deemed socially desirable. He expected that by midyear $317 billion in outstanding loans would be tied to credit or loan-guarantee programs administered or sponsored by the federal government. In addition to those specific programs, the government was also allocating credit through its budget.[6]

Other measures are hard to classify as negative or positive. Restrictions on their other loans and investments prod mutual savings banks and savings and loan associations into making mortgage loans (as well as into buying government and agency securities). Interest-rate ceilings under state usury laws and federal mortgage guarantee programs are presumably meant to protect borrowers; yet, like commodity price controls that cause shortages, they can harm would-be borrowers as lenders either divert their funds into uncontrolled uses or require bigger down payments and shorter maturities to reduce risks to levels commensurate with the controlled interest rates.

Under Regulation Q the Federal Reserve limits the interest rates that commercial banks may pay on time and savings deposits. Other regulatory agencies gained similar power over mutual savings banks and savings and loan associations in 1966.[7] Originally, it seems, these regulations were meant to restrain competition for deposits on the theory that banks would otherwise seek high earnings from excessively risky loans and investments. In the 1960s Regulation Q evolved into an instrument of monetary control. A change, from either side, in the spread between deposit interest

---

[5] Calculated from *Economic Report of the President Together with the Annual Report of the Council of Economic Advisers* (Washington, D.C.: U.S. Government Printing Office, January 1977), p. 264.

For a broader view of federal credit programs, see Dan Larkins, *$300 Billion in Loans* (Washington, D.C.: American Enterprise Institute for Public Policy Research, 1972).

[6] U.S., Congress, House of Representatives, Subcommittee on Domestic Monetary Policy of the Committee on Banking, Currency and Housing, *Hearings on an Act to Lower Interest Rates and Allocate Credit*, 94th Congress, 1st session, February 1975, p. 21 (hereafter cited as U.S., Congress, *Hearings*).

[7] Harry D. Hutchinson, *Money, Banking, and the United States Economy*, 3rd ed. (Englewood Cliffs, N.J.: Prentice-Hall, 1975), p. 179n., and Peter Fortune, "Discussion," in Federal Reserve Bank of Boston, *Credit Allocation Techniques and Monetary Policy* (1973), p. 45 (hereafter cited as FRBB, *Techniques*).

ceilings and open-market interest rates tends (though perhaps not strongly) to affect supplies of money and credit. A fall in deposit rates relative to market rates discourages people from holding time deposits. Given the total volume of bank reserves, decreased use of time deposits increases the portion of the total reserves available to support demand deposits. A relative rise in deposit rates, conversely, tends to shift bank reserves toward supporting time deposits and away from demand deposits.

Furthermore, when Regulation Q permits a relative rise in deposit rates, the share of total credit channeled through credit institutions rather than through the open market tends to increase. Since these institutions make loans and investments of various kinds in proportions that differ from those made by lenders and investors in the money and capital markets, a selective effect results. Credit terms ease in sectors where the deposit institutions are most active and tighten in other sectors. When deposit-rate ceilings fall relative to other interest rates available to savers, these selective effects work in the opposite direction, disadvantaging borrowers particularly dependent on banks and other deposit institutions.[8] This shift toward direct money-market transactions and away from channeling funds through the deposit institutions is known as disintermediation.

Since 1966, the regulators have generally set slightly lower ceilings for savings deposits at commercial banks than at mutual savings banks and savings and loan associations. The impediment to channeling funds through the banks has tended—though probably not powerfully—to favor the chief borrowing customers of the other institutions, that is, mortgage borrowers.[9]

The Federal Reserve tried to use Regulation Q more specifically in 1966. In September, when interest rates on money-market instruments rose above the ceiling rates on commercial banks' time and savings deposits and certificates of deposit, the Federal Reserve held those ceilings firm. By doing so, as well as by increasing reserve requirements against large certificates of deposit in July and September, it sought to protect the home-finance institutions from commercial-bank competition for deposits and also to restrict the flow of credit through big banks to big businesses. The use, not

---

[8] See Charles F. Haywood, *Regulation Q and Monetary Policy* (Chicago: Association of Reserve City Bankers, 1971), p. 27.

[9] Thomas D. Simpson, *Money, Banking, and Economic Analysis* (Englewood Cliffs, N.J.: Prentice-Hall, 1976), p. 238, and Haywood, *Regulation Q*, p. 41. See also Board of Governors of the Federal Reserve System, *The Federal Reserve System: Purposes and Functions*, 6th ed. (Washington, D.C., 1974), p. 85.

8

the effectiveness, of Regulation Q is what concerns us here. Only one source of credit to business was directly affected, suggesting that any impact was concentrated on firms too small to float bonds or notes in the open market.[10] The home-finance institutions, also subject to interest ceilings, suffered in 1966 not primarily because commercial banks were competing their deposits away but because savers were shifting out of deposits into Treasury bills and other money-market paper.[11]

Demand (checking) deposits bear an interest-rate ceiling of zero, but this control is best discussed in a later context.

"Moral suasion," also known as "jawboning" and "open-mouth policy," generally has a selective intent. The Federal Reserve can hint at reprisals against bankers who ignore its requests—perhaps a chilly reception at the discount window, or a rough time with the bank examiners. In February 1929 it warned banks by letter against lending to stock-market speculators. A similar letter in September 1966 warned against unloading municipal bonds and expanding business loans. Restraints against foreign lending adopted in the mid-1960s were initially "voluntary." In 1973 the Committee on Interest and Dividends issued guidelines calling for discrimination in interest rates and credit availability against big businesses and in favor of small businesses, farmers, home buyers, and consumers. In September 1974 the Federal Reserve sent its member banks a set of loan guidelines, drafted by its Federal Advisory Council, designed to encourage mortgage and other favored loans while

---

[10] As an official publication acknowledges, the Federal Reserve held interest rates on certificates of deposit at uncompetitive levels in relation to market rates "in an attempt to exert pressure on the banks that were most responsible for making loans to large corporate businesses. As a result, businesses began to place increasing reliance on obtaining funds in the commercial paper and bond markets, sources of funds that are not readily available to such borrowers as small businesses and consumers. The result of these developments was a great deal of churning in financial markets, a loss to some degree of the stability in financial flows and risk-taking associated with financial intermediation, and perhaps a disproportionate credit squeeze on those bank customers unable to shift to open-market sources of funds." Board of Governors, *Federal Reserve System*, pp. 85-86. The passage quoted refers to episodes in 1966 and 1969-1970.

[11] Jack M. Guttentag, "Selective Credit Controls on Residential Mortgage Credit," in *Studies*, ed. Kaminow and O'Brien, pp. 61-62 and footnote; Donald R. Hodgman, *Selective Credit Controls in Western Europe* (Chicago: Association of Reserve City Bankers, 1976), p. 5; and Fortune, "Discussion," in FRBB, *Techniques*, p. 45. It may count as still another selective credit control that, in a further effort to check such disintermediation, the Treasury in 1970 raised the smallest denomination of Treasury bill from $1,000 to $10,000.

discouraging loans for supposedly speculative and other disfavored purposes. Earlier that year Federal Reserve Chairman Burns wrote to the presidents of four Federal Reserve Banks asking them to remind commercial bankers in their districts of the credit needs of operators of cattle-feeding lots. The Federal Reserve also supposedly encouraged banks to lend to Real Estate Investment Trusts for projects which, with hindsight, turned out to be unwise.[12]

In December 1969 Congress enacted a far-reaching law giving the President standby powers to authorize the Federal Reserve to "regulate and control any and all extensions of credit" when he deems such action appropriate for controlling inflation. Allowing the President broad discretion, the act does not specify what categories of credit are to receive priority status. While remaining on the books, the act has so far not been called into use.[13]

Unsatisfied with granting mere standby authority, several members of Congress have introduced bills to mandate credit allocation. H.R. 3161, introduced in February 1975, called on the President to "allocate credit away from inflationary uses, and toward national priority uses." The President could delegate his powers under the bill to the Federal Reserve or any other appropriate agency. The Federal Reserve might steer credit towards priority uses not only by using its existing powers but also by imposing differential supplementary reserve requirements against bank loans and investments. The President might also, at his discretion, require banks "to adopt a voluntary affirmative action program encompassing a shift from the non-national priority category to the national priority category, or from the inflationary category to the noninflationary category."[14] This bill was superseded in May 1975 by a milder one, Representative Reuss's H.R. 6676, the Credit Uses Reporting Act of 1975. It designated a wide variety of priority

---

[12] U.S., Congress, *Hearings*, pp. 209-15, 274-75. Some legislators tried to make much of those instances, arguing in effect that since the Federal Reserve had already been allocating credit in questionable ways, the law might as well require it to make socially desirable allocations. Chairman Burns disputed whether his letter amounted to allocating credit to the meat industry. On moral suasion, see Simpson, *Money, Banking*, pp. 240-41; Randall C. Merris, "Credit Allocation and Commercial Banks," Federal Reserve Bank of Chicago, *Business Conditions* (August 1975), p. 16; and Guttentag, "Mortgage Credit," p. 62n. On the Federal Reserve letter of September 1966, see Sherman J. Maisel, *Managing the Dollar* (New York: Norton, 1973), pp. 102-5.

[13] Merris, "Credit Allocation," p. 16, and Board of Governors, *Federal Reserve System*, p. 90.

[14] Quoted in Hodgman, *Western Europe*, p. 4. It sounds like Orwellian Newspeak to "require" a "voluntary" program.

credit uses and instructed the Federal Reserve to define its provisions in more operational terms. Earlier references to voluntary credit allocation and priority uses were deleted; but a ninth category, "all other extensions of credit," was added to the list of types of credit on which large banks were to file reports. Although the bill would not have instituted actual credit allocation, critics contended that the required reporting would be a first step in that direction. It met defeat in the House of Representatives in June 1975.[15]

Senator Schweiker introduced S. 887, the Interest Reduction and Credit-Priority Act of 1975. Under its terms, every creditor or class of creditors should make no less than one-third of its extensions of credit for any of several noble-sounding purposes listed in the bill.

The Humphrey-Hawkins Bill (S. 50, the Full Employment and Balanced Growth Act of 1976) contained a sweeping provision calling for "A monetary policy designed to assure such rate of growth in the Nation's money supply, such interest rates, and such credit availability, including policies of credit reform, allocation, and international capital flows as are conducive to achieving and maintaining the full employment, production, purchasing power and priority goals specified" earlier in the bill.

What purposes or economic sectors are favored in typical proposals for credit allocation? Housing (especially for low- and moderate-income families), small businesses, farming, and state and local government are popular candidates. H.R. 6676 (the Credit Uses Reporting Act of 1975) implicitly gave priority status to "productive capital investment," farms and small business firms, housing, and other purposes, including "the accommodation of consumer credit needs basic to a rising standard of living for American families." Senator Schweiker's S. 887 added the following: "The provision of capital for investment in plant and equipment where necessary to assure adequate supplies of essential commodities"; "The provision of capital for investment necessary to create new jobs, prevent unemployment, or inflationary prices"; and "Such additional purposes as the Board [of Governors of the Federal Reserve System] determines to be appropriate in order to assure stable and balanced economic growth by the most efficient use of available credit." Such rhetoric sounds noble but is short on clear operational meaning.

Favoring some uses or users of credit means putting others at

---

[15] Merris summarizes the bills of January, February, and May 1975 in his "Credit Allocation," p. 17.

a disadvantage. These others presumably include supposedly speculative or inflationary activities, such as construction of gambling casinos or of office skyscrapers destined to stand empty. Low social priority is often accorded to loans to large corporations.

Weapons of Selective Credit Control

Our survey of past measures and recent proposals has shown several of the tools, weapons, or devices that might be employed to guide flows of credit. Under the most extreme approach, government officials would screen all loans, investments, borrowings, and security issues, forbidding some and requiring others. (For simplicity, lenders, borrowers, and transactions of less than specified sizes might be exempt.) This polar case of detailed prohibitions and commands may seem like a straw man; yet it is useful to have in mind when we consider how far in this direction an allocation program might drift as the regulators and Congress sought to plug loopholes.

A less extreme approach would require each controlled institution to hold no less than a specified fraction of its portfolio in loans and investments of officially favored types or no more than a specified fraction in disfavored types, or both.[16] These floors and ceilings might apply to entire portfolios or to changes from base positions. H.R. 212 would have authorized the Federal Reserve to require each bank to submit a target portfolio for future dates, showing shifts in loans and investments toward priority uses.[17]

Approaches of a still less extreme type would offer inducements rather than issue commands. Government loan guarantees are a familiar example. In addition to non-interest-bearing reserves related to their deposits, banks and other institutions might be required to hold supplementary reserves specified as percentages of their nonpriority loans and investments. Loans and investments of favored types, on the other hand, could reduce the volume of reserves otherwise required. These supplementary reserve requirements against nonpriority portfolio items and reserve reductions

---

[16] Lester Thurow has suggested requiring *every* financial institution to hold no less than a specified fraction of its asset portfolio in loans and investments of designated types—housing loans, perhaps—or, failing that, in a non-interest-bearing account with the government. Lester Thurow, "Proposals for Rechanneling Funds to Meet Social Priorities," in Federal Reserve Bank of Boston, *Policies for a More Competitive Financial System*, 1972, p. 181 (hereafter cited as FRBB, *Policies*).

[17] Testimony of Congressman Jim Wright in U.S., Congress, *Hearings*, pp. 7-8.

for favored ones might be calculated as percentages either of total holdings of the specified loans and investments or of changes in holdings beyond specified base amounts.

Foreign authorities have made some use of differential discount rates or privileges.[18] The central bank might rediscount favored loans at an exceptionally low interest rate. (The Federal Reserve Act of 1913 embodied a similar idea by making only certain types of loan ordinarily eligible for rediscounting, namely, short-term self-liquidating commercial and industrial loans and loans to agriculture.) Nonpriority loans could be rediscounted either not at all or only on penalty terms.

The government might establish special institutions to finance favored activities, like those favoring agriculture and housing in the United States. Latin American "fomentos" form another example, as do the World Bank and international development banks for particular regions. Savings banks might be required to channel portions of their depositors' funds into a governmental superbank; or, as in Sweden, contributions to private and public pension plans might be channeled into priority uses through a government institution. Several prominent American businessmen have proposed a reincarnation of the Reconstruction Finance Corporation (created in 1932 to aid distressed banks and railroads) to steer funds in officially favored directions.[19]

Usury laws and Regulation Q might be generalized into a comprehensive system of ceilings and floors on loan and deposit interest rates. Selectively wielded, such controls could promote some and deter other flows of credit. The controllers would have to guard against perverse effects: interest ceilings that encourage attempts to borrow might repel lenders and shrivel actual loans of the favored types, as has occurred with ceilings on mortgage interest rates. Regulation of interest rates and other credit terms is a particularly indirect and imprecise weapon, worth mentioning only for the sake of completeness.

Actually, completeness is impossible. The field is wide open for feats of routine originality in inventing new controls or modifications. The essence of the proposals is clear: to steer credit toward some uses and users and away from others by issuing commands and prohibitions or offering positive and negative inducements to

[18] Peter G. Fousek, *Foreign Central Banking: The Instruments of Monetary Policy* (New York: Federal Reserve Bank of New York, 1957), esp. pp. 13-30, 70-71.

[19] Walter E. Grinder and Alan Fairgate, "The Reconstruction Finance Corporation Rides Again," *Reason,* July 1975, pp. 23-29, esp. p. 23.

lenders and perhaps to borrowers also. This central idea is what we shall try to appraise.

Arguments for Controls and Their Weaknesses

What is the case for putting that idea into practice? No one seems to have worked out a systematic and coherent case,[20] but several arguments are in circulation. Hardly an argument is the pervasive feeling that some uses of credit are worthier than others and that therefore the government should take charge.

Imperfect Markets and Discrimination. More substantial arguments center on "imperfections" of the market.[21] Reality deviates from the well-organized competitive credit markets of abstract theory. Credit does not go straightforwardly to whichever borrowers agree to pay the prevailing interest rates. Instead, using additional criteria, lenders practice nonprice rationing. In granting and refusing loans, they *discriminate* as they see fit, perhaps in favor of big corporations and against new or small businesses, against poor people, and against people living or doing business in "redlined" sections of cities.[22]

---

[20] "Professional economic literature is devoid of any general theory of credit and credit controls as instruments of public policy. . . . Articles have appeared on the effects of various interest-rate ceilings. . . . But a thorough search in standard bibliographic sources reveals very little of a more general theoretical nature." Donald R. Hodgman, "Selective Credit Controls," *Journal of Money, Credit and Banking*, vol. 4 (May 1972), pp. 343-44.

[21] For an example of such arguments, as well as of the externality, merit want, and equity arguments to be reviewed below, see Thurow, "Proposals," in FRBB, *Policies*, pp. 179-89.

[22] Redlining is the practice of refusing to make mortgage loans on property in entire neighborhoods believed to be deteriorating, regardless of the credit-worthiness of particular borrowers or the good condition of particular properties. The lenders' judgments, so complaints go, can be self-fulfilling: denial of loans contributes to the deterioration of neighborhoods and seems to justify lenders' wariness. *Business Week*, March 22, 1976, pp. 143-44, and Dwight M. Jaffee, "Housing Finance and Mortgage Market Policy," in Karl Brunner et al., *Government Credit Allocation* (San Francisco: Institute for Contemporary Studies, 1975), p. 117. In January 1977 the governor of New Jersey signed into law a bill banning redlining. The state banking commissioner is authorized to levy a fine of up to $5,000 on each occasion when a lending institution refuses to make a mortgage loan for supposedly arbitrary reasons of geography (*Wall Street Journal*, January 13, 1977, p. 34).

Discriminatory nonprice rationing allegedly becomes extreme when money and credit are generally tight; credit institutions maintain their lending to favored borrowers and concentrate the squeeze on small business, housing, state and local governments, and other worthy sectors of the economy. Advocates of controls engage in Monday-morning quarterbacking: big banks allocated enormous sums to build skyscraper office buildings in Manhattan and elsewhere, many of which then stood half empty, to overbuild luxury condominiums, to build gambling casinos in the Bahamas and shooting reserves in Kenya, and to speculate in foreign exchange all over the world.[23] Credit allocation is inevitable, say advocates of controls; the policy issue is whether it is to follow narrow and arbitrary private criteria or sound national priorities.

Some critics count it an imperfection of the free market that corporations do not pay out all their profits and depreciation allowances to their stockholders. If full payouts were required, stockholders could decide whether to reinvest their funds in the same corporations or elsewhere. The savings of the economy would then be allocated in the capital markets instead of being reinvested by self-interested corporate managements.[24] Such criticism overlooks the costs of financial transactions, the cost savings from internal finance, and the market tests that even internally financed firms must face.

Arguments centering on market imperfections and private credit rationing damn reality for being real. Of course information is incomplete and imperfect and transactions are costly in the credit markets, as in all markets. Of course price (interest rates) alone cannot govern credit allocation, since the price is to be paid and the loan repaid in the future. Lenders do not know—and so must judge as best they can at reasonable cost—which prospective borrowers will repay on schedule and which will go broke or prove dishonest. Because exhaustive individual investigations would cost too much, lenders must use clues from experience with the creditworthiness of classes of borrowers. "Nonprice rationing" and "discrimination" are rather loaded labels for necessary rules of thumb and for the unavoidably subjective element in lenders' judgments. Second guessing of private lenders is all too easy for critics who work with unreal standards of market perfection and do not put their own money on the line. If government officials controlled credit allocation, they too

---

[23] Congressman Henry Reuss in U.S., Congress, *Hearings*, p. 23.

[24] Thurow, "Proposals," in FRBB, *Policies*, p. 181, and in U.S., Congress, *Hearings*, p. 84. It is symptomatic that Thurow speaks of the "savings of the economy" as if they had no particular owners.

would have to employ rules of thumb and make somewhat arbitrary decisions.[25]

In private markets, credit is rationed partly by interest rates and partly by the judgments of lenders. (Depending on definitions of terms, however, one might deny that financial institutions really allocate credit. Like other business firms, they respond to the "allocation" demands of their customers.)[26] Allocation by lenders, even if that is what it is, is decentralized, not monopolized. Someone denied credit by one lender still may get it from others, or get it indirectly, as a small businessman may obtain trade credit from his suppliers. If strong demand exists for some good or service whose production happens to be underfinanced, the profit motive will spur people to arrange financing in some way or other. Innovation in finance, as in other services and products, is a characteristic feature of a free economy.

This is not to say that free-market allocation of credit (or of anything else) is unbiased, neutral, or optimal. Such a claim would be absurd because nobody can specify an "optimal" allocation in concrete terms and because markets, like governments, have undeniable "warts." The imperfections and dispersion of knowledge and the costs of mobilizing it, the costs of conducting transactions and enforcing contracts, the impressionableness and prejudices and even downright cussedness of human beings—all of these characterize private enterprise and government alike. The case for allowing markets to function does not rest on assumptions about perfect competition and other imaginary conditions. Instead, it answers the question whether, on the whole, it is better to leave the task of coping with the warts of reality to decentralized private decisions or to central direction.

Discriminatory Tight Money. Discrimination among borrowers grows worse, say advocates of controls, when money tightens—when inter-

---

[25] Neither with nor without selective controls could monetary policy achieve ideal perfection. "Merely to show that one of these policies is not perfect . . . is not sufficient to build a case for its rival. It is hardly fair to compare an ideal model of one policy with an actual working model of the other policy." Thomas Mayer, "Financial Guidelines and Credit Controls," *Journal of Money, Credit and Banking*, vol. 4 (May 1972), p. 362.

[26] Government policy, in the opinion of the executive vice president of the Conference of State Bank Supervisors, should strive to make financial institutions still more responsive to the credit-allocation and financial-service demands of consumers and business firms, instead of telling the institutions and their customers what those demands should be. Lawrence E. Kreider, letter in U.S., Congress, *Hearings*, p. 366.

est rates rise and loans become harder to get, either because booming business conditions (and perhaps a federal government deficit) have strengthened demands for credit or because the Federal Reserve has tightened its policy. General monetary policy has sectoral or selective effects of sometimes doubtful merit.

The fact that some types of loan shrivel (or suffer curtailed growth) in greater proportion than others, however, is no proof of discrimination. Suppose that either credit or lumber somehow becomes scarcer relative to demand, causing its price to rise. Even in the most perfect of markets, extensions of credit or shipments of lumber would not decline in the same proportion to all users. The use of credit or of lumber is more postponable or more dispensable for some users than for others (thanks, perhaps, to better possibilities of substitution). Ultimate consumers will find some high-credit-content or high-lumber-content goods more postponable, replaceable, or dispensable than others and will respond accordingly as prices come to include the increased cost of credit or of lumber. Some direct business users and indirect consumers of credit or lumber will respond more sensitively than others to the worsened price and nonprice terms on which they can get credit or lumber.[27]

If credit or lumber use in one sector of the economy should respond quite sensitively as price and other terms improved or worsened, that very responsiveness would suggest (though not prove) that expansion or cutback of activity caused relatively little hardship to the persons involved.[28] In other sectors, where fluctuations would cause greater hardship, people would respond only sluggishly to changes in market terms. If, then, an overall tightening of money and credit affects loans to different borrowers and for different purposes in different degrees, this differential responsiveness does not prove that something is amiss. It results from give and take between thousands of financial institutions and their customers, whose decisions take account of their own special knowledge. It

---

[27] Does the point at issue here hold true even if the tighter rationing of credit or lumber takes place partly by worsened nonprice terms or tighter screening by suppliers rather than by higher price alone? Some considerations suggest that it does hold. Suppliers would hardly benefit from concentrating cutbacks on those economic sectors that would suffer most. A mere reference to monopoly does not refute the point. Even if the supply of credit or lumber were monopolized, what better form than price would the monopolist have in which to collect his monopoly gain?

[28] Housing may well be such a sector. Workers can shift between housing and other types of construction; the seasonal nature of their work encourages them to maintain contacts with alternative employments. And consumers can postpone their moves into better housing.

suggests that the millions of people directly and indirectly involved are responding appropriately in view of their own particular circumstances. Since not as much credit or capital is available as people want at some previous, lower, interest rate, some uses must be curtailed. A rise in interest rates will, by and large, curtail uses in such a way as to minimize hardship. Each would-be borrower estimates the extent of hardship for himself and decides whether paying to avoid it is worth his while. The hardship of doing without credit might be great for some uses in some categories, yet small for other uses in the same category. Emotionalism about supposed hardship in worthy economic sectors is thus a poor basis for policy. Yet any administrative allocation program normally rations credit by category. It cannot allow for the fact that hardships from failure to obtain credit may well differ more from use to use within categories than from category to category. Government allocation of credit, based on outsiders' notions about appropriate flows of credit, would make much useful knowledge go to waste.[29] Locking all flows of credit into fixed proportions with each other would make an overall tightening of money and credit work in a nondiscriminatory fashion only on a most superficial view.

These considerations do not, of course, prove the absence of discrimination in any bad sense of the word. Bach and Huizenga tried to grapple with some aspects of the factual issue. During the period of tight money or credit running from October 1955 to October 1957, bank loans to large borrowers did increase much more than loans to small borrowers. Bach and Huizenga looked not just at the actual pattern of loans, however, but at the suppliers' side of the market. They developed measures for classifying banks as "loose" or "tight" according to whether their lendable funds were ample or scanty. Comparison suggests, by and large, that banks especially squeezed for funds did not especially restrict credit to small borrowers. They tended to stick with their regular criteria of creditworthiness. Insofar as they did discriminate to a limited extent on other bases, bankers seemed to take particular care of their best customers—large businesses at large banks and small businesses at small banks. Bach and Huizenga agreed with the conclusion of a Federal Reserve study that the demand for bank credit rose less rapidly between 1955 and 1957 by small businesses than by large ones; this seemed to be the main reason for the differential growth

[29] On how the price system mobilizes knowledge, including even the knowledge that people have about their own local and temporary circumstances, see F. A. Hayek, "The Use of Knowledge in Society," *American Economic Review*, vol. 35 (September 1945), pp. 519-30.

in loans. Banks increased their loans the most to those firms whose business was expanding most rapidly and in those sectors of the economy where the investment boom was strongest. Another indication that tight money did not especially discriminate against small business borrowers is that those firms received trade credit from their larger suppliers in greatly expanded amounts. [30]

This study drew some criticism.[31] Bach and Huizenga tacitly assumed that borrowers' loan demand remained substantially the same at loose and tight banks of different asset sizes. In fact, borrowers might have shifted from banks that could not meet their credit demands to banks that could. Furthermore, actual volumes of loans reflect some combination of supply and demand factors, yet behavior on the supply side is what the issue of discrimination is all about. Silber and Polakoff attempted an improved analysis of that behavior. They used data for 1955 and 1957 of the same general sort that Bach and Huizenga had used—but only for the New York Federal Reserve district, a district hardly typical of the country at large. They fitted supposed supply functions, taking individual banks as the units of observation in cross-section regressions. The dependent variables were volumes of loans to borrowers of various asset sizes; the independent variables were deposits, average interest rates and maturities of loans, and fractions of loans that were secured. The ratios of the coefficient of the deposit term in regressions for 1955, the year of relatively easier money, to the same coefficient for the tight-money year 1957 generally declined with increasing size-class of borrower. Silber and Polakoff took this as evidence of a desire to discriminate against small borrowers in times of tight money. Their methodology and conclusions in turn came under attack.[32]

---

[30] G. L. Bach and C. J. Huizenga, "The Differential Effects of Tight Money," *American Economic Review*, vol. 51 (March 1961), pp. 52-80. For further discussion of the variety of sources of credit available to small business firms, including credit through informal channels not adequately covered in published statistics, see Irving Schweiger, "Adequacy of Financing for Small Business since World War II," *Journal of Finance*, vol. 13 (September 1958), pp. 323-47.

[31] G. L. Bach reviews and answers the early criticism and extends the work of the original study in "How Discriminatory Is Tight Money?" in *Banking and Monetary Studies*, ed. Deane Carson (Homewood, Ill.: Irwin, 1963), pp. 254-90.

[32] Wlliam L. Silber and Murray E. Polakoff, "The Differential Effects of Tight Money: An Econometric Study," *Journal of Finance*, vol. 25 (March 1970), pp. 83-97; Jonas Prager and Jacob Paroush, "On the Differential Effects of Tight

The discussion shows disagreement and confusion about the very concept of discrimination; statistics alone are no substitute for appropriate conceptualization. The disagreement and confusion suggest that the evil in question, if it exists at all, is not a gross and palpable one. Such a doubtful and poorly diagnosed evil is hardly a prime candidate for governmental remedies. Even if discrimination could be shown to occur in some sense or other of the word, that fact would not in itself mean that the government could or should do something about it.

The idea prevails widely that general monetary restraint discriminates against housing construction. That sector has indeed shown greater cyclical variability since World War II than most other components of GNP. During years of peak general prosperity, usually accompanied by tight credit, housing construction generally drops, typically ahead of the general business downturn. During the credit crunch of 1966, "housing starts dropped to a 20-year low despite a record number of family formations; sales of existing homes fell off, and a great many contractors and realtors went out of business." During or shortly after the downward phase of the business cycle, on the other hand, home building typically revives. Many observers attribute this cyclical variability partly to the trouble that the major mortgage lenders, savings and loan associations and mutual savings banks, have in competing for funds as interest rates rise. Their deposit-interest ceilings pose one source of trouble. Another is that their interest earnings lag because the mortgages in their portfolios have long maturities. Furthermore, the demand for housing and for mortgage loans is more sensitive to interest rates than demands in other sectors of the economy. Interest forms a larger share of total expenditure in buying homes than in buying less long-lived goods. Families can more easily postpone buying new houses than business firms can postpone making investments, since a firm often risks losing its share of the market if it does not improve and add to its plant and equipment.[33]

Before hastening to put the blame on "tight money" or general monetary restraint, we should distinguish between rising interest rates and restraint on growth of the money supply. They are not the same thing. Excessively fast money-supply growth tends, after

Money: A Comment," pp. 951-54, and Silber and Polakoff, "Reply," pp. 955-58, both in *Journal of Finance*, vol. 26 (September 1971).

[33] Lawrence S. Ritter and William L. Silber, *Principles of Money, Banking, and Financial Markets* (New York: Basic Books, 1974), pp. 421-28. Compare Chase Manhattan Bank, "Housing and Inflation," *Business in Brief*, June 1976, pp. 4-5.

a period of opposite impact, to raise interest rates through its effect on prices and price expectations.[34] The three occasions over the years 1951-1967 when the housing sector's share of gross national product underwent a prolonged decline were all times of substantial rather than slow or negative monetary growth. Housing has suffered at times of slow monetary growth, though not much more than economic activity in general; and on several occasions of monetary restraint, the decline in housing starts reversed itself after three to six months. The decline in interest rates that results ultimately (not immediately) from a shift from excessive to moderate monetary growth actually stimulates housing. This, anyway, is the conclusion reached by Norman Bowsher and Lionel Kalish III. In their judgment, both financial institutions and the housing industry, like other sectors, flourish best in an economy growing at a relatively steady rate without inflation.[35]

The perceptions of Bowsher and Kalish have remained applicable in the years since they wrote. If housing's problems are financial in origin, the financial problem traces in turn to inflation. The Chase Manhattan Bank, in a mid-1976 publication, made that diagnosis of "the recurring financial problem of the past decade. Mortgage interest rates frequently seemed 'too high' to the public—and yet weren't high enough to bring forth the amount of credit borrowers wanted at those rates, let alone the amount needed to build housing at the pace many people thought necessary." Uptrends in the inflation rate and consequently in interest rates have troubled mortgage lenders, who typically borrow short and lend long. Inflation contributed to the 1973-1974 housing slump partly by eroding people's ability to afford new housing and partly by curtailing the

[34] Eugene F. Fama, "Short-Term Interest Rates as Predictors of Inflation," *American Economic Review*, vol. 65 (June 1975), pp. 269-82; David I. Fand, "The 69-70 Slowdown," *Financial Analysts Journal* (January-February 1971); William E. Gibson, "Interest Rates and Monetary Policy," *Journal of Political Economy*, vol. 78 (May/June 1970), pp. 431-55; and D. G. Taylor, *The Effects of Monetary Growth on the Interest Rate* (Ph.D. diss., University of Chicago, 1973).

[35] Norman Bowsher and Lionel Kalish III, "Does Slower Monetary Expansion Discriminate against Housing?" Federal Reserve Bank of St. Louis, *Review*, vol. 50 (June 1968), pp. 5-12. This article, along with Bach and Huizenga's "Differential Effects" and other studies, is cited favorably in Mayer, "Financial Guidelines," pp. 360-74. Mayer reviews data and studies bearing on the view that a general tight-money policy discriminates against housing and against investment by state and local governments and in favor of business investment and consumer credit. The evidence, he concludes, does not bear out this view.

availability and escalating the cost of mortgage credit. "The key element in the improvement of the housing market since 1974 is the halving of the inflation rate and the reduction of inflationary expectations." Introduction of variable-interest-rate mortgages might be helpful by reducing risks to lenders, but an enduring solution "must center on lowering the long-term rate of inflation." Otherwise, housing finance "will remain a chronic problem and further Topsy-like growth of the Government's role will be likely."[36]

To recognize that housing has been plagued by financial vicissitudes, including spurts and slumps in money-supply growth, inflation, and interest rates, is not the same as maintaining that the volume of construction over the long run depends strongly on the terms and availability of credit through particular channels. That is a rather different question, considered in chapter 2.

One more thing remains to be said about "discriminatory" impacts on particular economic sectors. If it is desirable that monetary policy should switch between tightness and ease to affect total spending in the economy, then it is unavoidable, and indeed appropriate, that these switches should have differential impacts. Only by fantastic coincidence could all sectors of the economy be equally responsive to changes in credit terms and other market conditions; and there is some presumption, as argued a few pages earlier, that a relatively sensitive response implies a relatively less painful response. Monetary policy needs "handles" with which to get a grip on the economy. As Lawrence Ritter and William Silber said about housing, "It is not such a bad thing, once you think about it, for the economy to have a foul weather friend"—a sector that slackens in boom periods and revives during recessions.[37] Stanley Diller has developed a similar argument. The services of owner-occupied houses remain much the same from year to year, while the value of machines and business inventories is volatile. In a boom, postponement of house buying under the influence of increased interest rates is a

---

[36] Chase Manhattan Bank, *Housing and Inflation*, pp. 4-5. The quoted passages have been rearranged here and the original paragraphing ignored.

[37] Ritter and Silber, *Principles of Money, Banking*, p. 426. This is not to say, of course, that housing is the only sector responsive to credit terms and general monetary policy. For a discussion of the responsiveness of spending on consumer durable goods, see Paul F. Smith, "Controlling the Terms on Consumer Credit," in FRBB, *Techniques*, pp. 52ff. In partial contrast, a paper by Hamburger and Zwick, to be discussed below, emphasizes uncertainty about the working of consumer credit terms and controls. The disagreement prevailing on these issues underlines the unpredictability of the results of extending government power still further.

rational response to economic realities and is even a favorable development for the economy. It reduces competition for real resources as well as for credit, permitting business investment to keep on expanding longer than it otherwise would. Real income benefits; and so, ultimately, does the demand for houses.[38]

The preceding discussion concerns the acceptability of differential impacts if it is deemed desirable that general monetary policy should switch between tightness and ease. If the results are discriminatory in a bad sense of the term, it is the switches that are at fault. Discrimination does not result from the money supply's simply being of one size rather than another or from its simply growing at one steady rate rather than another. The selective effects of general monetary policy result from its zigzagging between tightness and ease; and if the monetary authorities deplore those effects, they should avoid the zigzags.[39] One might reply that changes in the tightness of money and credit are due to the business cycle rather than policy. There is no denying, though, that the authorities do deliberately change their policy from time to time. To the extent, furthermore, that major swings in the business cycle represent lagged responses to earlier zigzags in policy, the blame for unwanted selective effects remains on those zigzags. A steadier policy might be a better remedy than government credit allocation.[40]

Support of Macro Policy. Although no one, to my knowledge, has so argued in detail, one might conceivably want selective credit controls as an aid to macroeconomic stabilization policy. Controls over

---

[38] Sanford Rose summarizes Diller's argument in "Why Fannie, Ginnie, and Freddy Can't Do It," *Fortune*, March 1977, pp. 111, 113-14. The same general theme—that "[h]ousing is an eminently postponable purchase" and that housing is a suitable "handmaiden" of monetary policy—is developed in William E. Gibson, "Protecting Homebuilding from Restrictive Credit Conditions," *Brookings Papers on Economic Activity*, no. 3 (Washington, D.C.: Brookings Institution, 1973), pp. 647-91, followed by comments and discussion.

[39] Recall Bowsher and Kalish's remark in favor of steady growth without inflation, and compare Otto Eckstein's reason for favoring a program of credit allocation. If the Federal Reserve is to manage aggregate demand by large doses of monetary restraint, then it must face the consequences and allocate credit. If it were to manage demand in a more moderate way (which Eckstein does not expect), then the country's good capital market and wide range of financial institutions would successfully channel savings to productive investment purposes. Eckstein, letter in U.S., Congress, *Hearings*, pp. 296-97.

[40] Just how monetary policy should be measured or gauged and just what a *steady* policy might consist of are questions rather far afield from the topic of this study. Suffice it to say that the rate of growth of the quantity of money has much to do with the answers.

cyclically unstable flows of spending—business investment and consumer spending on durable goods, for example—might serve to keep those components of total expenditure from infecting other sectors of the economy. But do selective controls merely change the shape and composition of aggregate spending, or do they work directly to alter that aggregate? One of the opposing extreme positions on this question is the "someone else will use the money" school: If someone is kept from borrowing, someone else will use the available loanable funds. Pushing a balloon into a different shape does not change its size. At the other extreme, the "additive" school assumes that since a total is the sum of its parts, changing one or more of them—reducing expenditure on automobiles, for example—will obviously change the total.[41]

The balloon (or someone-else) theory might conceivably be correct at a time of excess aggregate demand, and the additive theory might be correct in recession. During periods of strong expansionary pressures, selective controls could, at best, alter the composition of total spending. Only in recession could they help hold down total spending. In short, selective controls could restrain total spending not when restraint would be appropriate but only when it would be inappropriate.[42] History recommends skepticism, furthermore, about whether the processes of politics, bureaucracy, and economic forecasting would achieve suitable *timing* of selective credit controls. Congress reinstated controls on installment buying in September 1948, just as the economy was about to tip from boom into recession.

One rather weak argument for selective credit controls—especially of obvious kinds, as on consumer credit—is that the general public finds them more understandable than the mysteries of open-market operations and that this helps make them politically feasible. Part of the obvious answer is that the problem with macroeconomic policy is not a lack of weapons, but inconsistency and unsteadiness of purpose in their use. A proliferation of control weapons impedes public understanding of and support for the few weapons that really count.[43] A further reply would emphasize that what we really want

---

[41] Paul F. Smith, "Terms on Consumer Credit," in FRBB, *Techniques*, pp. 51-52.

[42] Paul F. Smith, "Consumer Credit Controls," in *Studies*, ed. Kaminow and O'Brien, pp. 132-33. Smith is describing a theory on which, he says, there is no persuasive evidence one way or the other. He is considering, in particular, the possible use of consumer credit controls for macroeconomic stabilization.

[43] Robert C. Turner, "A Comment on the Need for Consumer Credit Controls," selection #29, esp. p. 220, and Milton Friedman, "Consumer Credit Control as an Instrument of Stabilization Policy," selection #28, pp. 195-216, both

in policy measures is appropriateness, not short-run political acceptability based on a deficient grasp of reality.

Imperfections, Existing Controls, and Differential Impacts

Markets in the real world undeniably have imperfections, some of which cause tight money to have uneven effects on different sectors of the economy. Labor is not perfectly mobile. A defect in mortgage arrangements, which might be corrected, impairs the market for old houses. The owner of a house mortgaged at an interest rate below the current rate has an implicit gain which he cannot transfer to a buyer of the house if the mortgage itself is not transferable. The only practical way to keep his gain is not to sell the house. This obstacle to transactions in old houses presumably has some deterrent effect on new construction.

Furthermore, housing is generally financed more heavily with borrowed funds rather than are business corporations, which rely more on plowed-back profits for financing their investment projects. Even if a general tightening of credit and rise in interest rates makes plowing back profits less attractive than before in comparison with outside investments that a corporation might make or that its stockholders might make with money paid out as dividends, corporate bureaucrats, guided by self-interest, might go ahead with internally financed projects anyway. At least, this result is commonly alleged, given impairments to competition and the profit motive.[44] As a further result, the general credit squeeze has a disproportionate impact on economic activities that depend on borrowed funds. When interest rates rise markedly, savings and loan associations and savings banks are handicapped in competing for deposits by their heavy holdings of long-term mortgages bearing interest fixed at the old lower levels. Restrictions on the asset and liability choices of the savings institutions contribute to this problem.[45] With generally rising interest rates, the savings institutions would be squeezed between increased deposit interest payments (if allowed to make them) and their relatively constant interest earnings, which rise only gradually as their mortgage portfolios gradually turn over. Inflation, re-

---

in *Money and Economic Activity*, ed. Lawrence S. Ritter, 2nd ed. (Boston: Houghton Mifflin, 1961).

[44] See Mayer, "Financial Guidelines," pp. 368-69.

[45] Fortune, "Discussion," in FRBB, *Techniques*, p. 44, says that these restrictions have aggravated the housing cycle.

flected in interest rates, contributes to this difficulty.[46] Mutual savings banks and most savings and loan assocations are owned by their depositors rather than by stockholders. Any resultant weakening of pressures to seek maximum profits presumably allows their managers more scope for gratifying personal preferences and whims in allocating credit.

Some market imperfections are largely the result of existing controls, notably various interest ceilings and restrictions on mortgage and other loans and on the deposits of banks and thrift institutions.[47] As already mentioned, "disintermediation" at times of high open-market interest rates puts these institutions—and their borrowing customers—at a disadvantage.

Banks are forbidden to pay interest on demand (checking) deposits. This ban turns competition for deposits into nonprice channels. One of these other ways of rewarding big depositors seems to be preferential treatment when they want to borrow. This method of attracting deposits could go far toward explaining any apparent discrimination in favor of big and established business customers and against other loan applicants, particularly in times of tight money. Allowing banks to pay interest on demand deposits would reduce the extent to which competition for deposits takes the form of apparently discriminatory lending policies.[48]

In the view of some observers, the tax exemption of interest income earned on the bonds of state and local governments aggravates the cyclical instability of finance for these government units. A general rise in interest rates tends to reduce the attractiveness of

---

[46] Raymond Saulnier argues that inflation transforms the standard mortgage, which used to work so well to promote homeownership, into an obstacle to housing finance. "A Program to Moderate the Impact of Tight Money on the Home Mortgage Market," in *Savings and Residential Financing, 1970 Conference Proceedings*, ed. Donald P. Jacobs (Chicago: United States Savings and Loan League, 1970), esp. p. 105. Compare Bowsher and Kalish as cited earlier in this chapter. Introduction of variable-rate mortgages could conceivably alleviate this particular difficulty.

[47] See Mayer, "Financial Guidelines," as well as Bowsher and Kalish, "Slower Monetary Expansion," and Harmon H. Haymes, *An Investigation of the Alleged Discriminatory Impact of General Credit Controls in Periods of Monetary Stringency* (Ph.D. diss., University of Virginia, 1959), esp. chapters 3 and 7.

[48] Edward J. Kane persuasively makes this argument in "Discussion," in FRBB, *Policies*, pp. 190-91 and 194-95, and in "Deposit-Interest Ceilings and Sectoral Shortages of Credit: How to Improve Credit Allocation without Allocating Credit," in Brunner et al., *Government Credit Allocation*, pp. 19-20. Of course, a valid argument for some policy change is not necessarily a *conclusive* argument.

the tax exemption, they argue, leading banks and other investors to shift their bond purchases elsewhere.[49]

Externalities and Merit Wants. Another line of argument for government credit allocation takes a leaf out of the book of academic theorists. It focuses on "externalities." External diseconomies and economies are damages and benefits that some people inflict or confer on others, who do not, however, ordinarily receive or pay compensation. Standard examples are the damage that a factory does by spewing smoke from its chimneys or dumping wastes into a river, or the agony that the barking of a dog inflicts on the neighbors, or the feelings of envy or inferiority that a man may arouse by driving an expensive new car. On the more cheerful side, an apple grower may unintentionally provide nectar for his neighbor's bees, a company's research for its own products may yield widely beneficial knowledge, or one man's care of his lawn may improve his entire neighborhood. In such cases, the signals transmitted by the price system are inaccurate. A person deciding on an activity that incidentally harms others will probably carry the activity "too far" (to the point where additions to the losses of all affected persons outweigh additions to their benefit), since he does not bear all of the true costs. A person deciding on an activity that incidentally benefits others will probably cut it "too short" (at a point where additions to the benefit of all affected persons would still outweigh additions to total costs), since not all the benefits accrue to him. Market prices misrepresent the true terms of choice between complete packages of net satisfactions.

Housing is a commonly cited example. Benefits radiate beyond the individual homeowner. Good housing supposedly lessens crime and juvenile delinquency. Homeownership supposedly contributes to neighborliness and good citizenship. Maintenance and landscaping improve the tone of the neighborhood; yet individual investors in rental housing or in their own homes would hold their investment down to the scale justified only by the benefits that they themselves expected to receive, not counting the external or "social" benefits. Renters would have even less reason to take account of such benefits. If assertions like these were valid,[50] there might be a case for government action to foster housing on a larger scale than the free

---

[49] Fortune, "Discussion," in FRBB, *Techniques*, pp. 43-44; Haymes, *Discriminatory Impact*, pp. 42-46, 158-60.

[50] The asserted externalities are not, in fact, well documented. Reasons exist for skepticism about the idea that poor housing breeds crime and disease. Poor housing, like crime and disease, may well be an effect of poverty, to

market would provide. Broadly similar arguments might call for government action to favor health services, research, energy conservation, education, the arts, and small and minority-owned businesses. Credit allocation could help favor activities radiating external benefits and restrict those radiating external costs.

Similarly, credit allocation might be used to promote satisfaction of "merit wants." Akin to external benefits, this concept is broader and looser. It refers to goods and services that people ought to be encouraged to consume in their own interest, even if their consumption did not radiate external benefits onto other people. The argument for favoring merit goods is paternalistic, resting on the tacit assumption that consumers do not fully appreciate what is good for them. Supposed merit goods include not only housing, education, and health care but also the arts and other elements of culture.[51] One might graft onto the merit-want argument the contention that consumers are deceived about their own interests by advertising and salesmanship and model changes—by appeals to snobbishness and faddishness.[52]

Externalities are prime theoretical examples of market "distortions" for which government policy could conceivably correct. Yet even in abstract theory, the mere existence of an externality does not mean the scale of the activity generating it is unambiguously too small or too large. This point hinges on a distinction between total and marginal external effects. On the whole, use of citizens' band radio by other drivers on the highways benefits the typical individual user: the others' use gives him free information and contacts. Yet this fact does not mean that CB usage is too small and ought to be subsidized. It might even be too large because, at the margin, it could be inflicting an external diseconomy in the form of congestion of the airwaves.[53] The principles of scarcity and general economic interdependence call for further skepticism about external-

which disease and personality disorders contribute. See Richard F. Muth, *Public Housing: An Economic Evaluation* (Washington, D.C.: American Enterprise Institute for Public Policy Research, 1973), esp. chapter 3.

[51] For an example of use of externality and merit-want arguments in favor of government credit allocation, see Thurow, "Proposals," in FRBB, *Policies*, esp. pp. 183-84. Richard A. Musgrave develops the concept of merit wants in *The Theory of Public Finance* (New York: McGraw-Hill, 1959), esp. pp. 13-14.

[52] See Turner, "Need for Consumer Credit Controls," as well as the many writings of John Kenneth Galbraith.

[53] This point, though not the particular example, is due to John H. Moore. James M. Buchanan and W. Craig Stubblebine do not quite make the same point, but they come close, in their "Externality," *Economica*, vol. 29 (November 1962), pp. 371-84.

ity arguments. Measures that divert resources into governmentally favored activities necessarily divert them from others. This obvious, indeed banal, point does not receive due attention because we seldom can specify just what the disadvantaged other activities are. For all we know, they might be ones generating external benefits at least as great as those generated by the favored activities. In the real world, externalities are all over the place, beneficial and harmful, trivial and not so trivial. Government attempts to correct for any large portion of them would prove futile, yet could cause economic, political, and social changes—changes in the direction of totalitarianism—far more harmful than the supposed corrections could justify. At any rate, important externalities create incentives for private parties to devise transactions or arrangements for taking them into account ("internalizing" them) after all.[54] For an economic theorist, it is a routine exercise to invoke externalities in an argument, formally valid on a certain level of abstraction, for almost any sort of government intervention plausible enough to command some political support.[55] To deserve being taken seriously, such an argument must center on one of the few externalities that are clearest, strongest, and most important, yet not amenable to nongovernmental remedies.

As argued later on,[56] the case for credit controls to remedy supposed distortions is strongest when the distortions are centered in the credit markets themselves instead of being of some other type. (In general, this is *not* true of the distortions cited in the externalities and merit-want arguments and in the redistribution argument still to be mentioned.) What sort of distortions might occur in the credit markets? Some, as already noted, might result from policy measures (such as interest-rate ceilings) that interfere with credit transactions. Additional measures might neutralize those interferences. In order to justify trying to steer credit toward students, one might cite not only the supposed external benefits of higher education [57] but also

---

[54] Internalization may be achieved if the relevant property rights have been clearly enough defined and if transaction costs are low enough. This is one of the themes of Ronald Coase, "The Problem of Social Cost," *Journal of Law and Economics*, vol. 3 (October 1960), pp. 1-44.

[55] George J. Stigler, "The Economists' Traditional Theory of the Economic Function of the State," *The Citizen and the State: Essays on Regulation* (Chicago: University of Chicago Press, 1975).

[56] See chapter 3, under "Where to Apply Corrective Measures."

[57] For perceptive and properly skeptical remarks on arguments for subsidies to higher education based on externalities or related effects, see Yale Brozen, "Foreword" to John J. Agria, *College Housing: A Critique of the Federal College Housing Loan Program* (Washington, D.C.: American Enterprise Institute for Public Policy Research, 1972).

the difficulty of pledging one's enhanced expected future income as security for a loan. Anyway, people who argue for remedying distortions should be clear about just what the distortions are, should advocate measures that apply to the points of distortion (including repeal of existing statutes and regulations that may be at fault), and should consider whether credit controls are more suitable than any alternative measures. A jumble of vague arguments, appealing to various *possibilities* of distortion, is not enough.

Fairness and Redistribution. Notions of "fairness" come into the case for government credit allocation.[58] In particular, such a program might help redistribute income and wealth—real purchasing power—from rich to poor people. For example, it might try to steer credit away from luxury housing and toward housing for low-income families.

Further appraisal of externality, merit-want, and redistribution or equity arguments is best left for a broader context. The last chapter of this study considers not so much the desirability of particular measures as whether it is the government's job to direct the national pattern of production and consumption in any manner. The prevalent attitude on this broad question does not hinge on sophisticated theoretical arguments. Rather, it seems to be an inarticulate feeling that everything good ought to be promoted and everything bad suppressed, primarily by the government. This feeling needs exposure and examination.[59]

Working through the Market. Meanwhile, let us note one final argument sometimes dredged up for preferring credit controls to measures of other kinds. Credit controls could work through the market, enlisting market incentives to favor some kinds of production and consumption over others. Blunt administrative orders are avoided; the impersonality and decentralization of the market economy remain. (Some supporters of a market economy apparently attribute this virtue to regulations or inducements affecting the loan and investment portfolios of financial institutions.)

---

[58] "Agriculture and small business would benefit from any general program to insure equitable treatment for the small, irregular, noncorporate borrower. . . ." Thurow, "Proposals," in FRBB, *Policies*, p. 183.

[59] George J. Stigler, *The Factors of Economic Reform*, Selected Papers, no. 13 (Chicago: Graduate School of Business, University of Chicago, 1964), reprinted in *The Citizen and the State*.

2

LOOPHOLES AND THEIR CONSEQUENCES

An appraisal of credit controls must examine how effective they are and whether they are likely to proliferate as the authorities strive to plug loopholes. Until now we have not questioned whether controls will indeed influence credit flows and production and consumption as intended. Now we must examine this assumption. We can hardly assert the contrary—that controls are totally ineffective—although they may produce the opposite of their intended results (as, for example, mortgage-rate ceilings may do). Anything that aids or impedes doing a particular thing in a particular way—like constructing race tracks with money borrowed from banks—will in principle have *some* effect on the scale of the activity. The costs of getting around controls will to some extent encourage compliance.[1] The real question concerns how strong, precise, durable, and generally worthwhile controls are. Are their effects significant and dependable enough to justify the costs involved? Beyond that, are governmental influences on production and consumption and on the distribution of income and wealth sufficiently desirable?

The suspicion that loopholes and costs will plague credit controls is not "merely theoretical." The purpose of theory is to subsume particular cases under broader categories, reducing the amount of

---

[1] Suppose that large firms are the targets of selective credit restriction. Even if the restriction endures long enough for firms to learn to cope with it, partly by resorting to new financial instruments and institutions, the target firms will not be able to escape its effects entirely unless they can find ways to obtain credit at marginal costs constant at the same level as would prevail in the absence of the restriction. John H. Wood, "Some Effects of Bank Credit Restrictions on the Short-Term Behavior of Large Firms," in *Studies in Selective Credit Policies*, ed. Ira Kaminow and James M. O'Brien (Philadelphia: Federal Reserve Bank of Philadelphia, 1975), p. 165.

case-by-case empiricism. The presumption that people will get around controls falls under a well-warranted generalization. Much experience shows that willing buyers and sellers of a good or service will find ways to trade with one another, despite obstacles—consider drugs, gambling, prostitution, and pornography. For at least two reasons, it should be easier to get around government credit restrictions. First, there are more alternative ways of providing finance than of providing drugs and the like. Second, credit transactions carry less of a moral stigma. Another well-warranted generalization also applies: Controls not conforming to the logic of a price system produce conditions that lead the controllers to call for tightening and extending the controls.

Fungibility

Regarding circumvention of selective credit controls, the *fungibility* of money and credit is a key concept. Something is fungible, says *The Random House Dictionary*, if it is "of such nature or kind as to be freely exchangeable or replaceable, in whole or in part, for another of like nature or kind." Money and grain are examples. Since the individual units are to all intents and purposes indistinguishable from one another, it is pointless or impossible to trace their comings and goings. This is particularly true for a business firm engaged in many different activities. It can obtain money from so many different sources and spend it for so many different purposes that one could seldom identify a particular dollar as being borrowed from a particular source and being spent for a particular purpose.

A perhaps apocryphal story illustrates this point. The Austrian government wanted to use some of the U.S. aid funds it was receiving after World War II to rebuild the Vienna Opera House. The Americans insisted that their aid was meant for more productive projects. So the Austrians obtained aid to build a hydroelectric plant and rebuilt the Opera with funds of their own that they had intended to spend on the hydroelectric plant. Now, is it meaningful to deny (or affirm) that American money financed the Opera?

Suppose, similarly, that a builder of homes for both low-income and high-income families obtains a bank loan. Which type of housing does the loan finance? Even if the builder knew in his own mind which type he would have curtailed if denied the loan, a credit-allocation program would give him reason not to tell the bank and would give the banker reason not to press for the information.

Policing could hardly be tight enough to make sure that a borrower does not use funds obtained for one stated purpose for some other purpose in fact. It would be all the harder to police business firms operating in several industries or financing a large part of their investments by plowing back profits.[2]

Individuals as well as corporations can exploit fungibility. The asset pledged as security for a loan may not be the one on which borrowed money is actually spent. Someone wanting to obtain funds for his small business or for buying corporation stock may mortgage his house. Government favoritism toward borrowing for housing may encourage consumers to incur more mortgage debt than they otherwise would—to increase the debt/equity ratio in their housing finance—and then pay cash for consumer goods they would otherwise have bought on credit.[3] Many owners can afford to pay for their houses without borrowing and will do so if mortgage interests rates are high. Controls that drive down mortgage interest rates, however, can make mortgage loans an attractive source of funds even for such things as cars, boats, and corporation stocks. At least two kinds of evidence suggest that this effect does occur. First, the economy's overall ratio of mortgage debt to housing investment does vary inversely with the mortgage interest rate. Second, surveys of consumer finance suggest that "wealthy families, holding already large portfolios of financial assets and consumer durables, find it expedient (profitable) to finance their homes not out of their own assets, but out of mortgage debt."[4]

Allan Meltzer has assembled further evidence. Despite long-standing policies in the United States and Western Europe of increasing the "availability" of mortgage credit, stocks of houses have grown over the long run at approximately the same rate as stocks of other assets and more slowly than the volume of outstanding mortgage debt. The ratio of housing to total assets remained unchanged while the ratios of mortgage debt to both housing and total liabilities rose markedly. Making credit "available" for housing seems to affect

2 Thomas Mayer, "Financial Guidelines and Credit Controls," *Journal of Money, Credit and Banking*, vol. 4 (May 1972), p. 81, and Randall C. Merris, "Credit Allocation and Commercial Banks," Federal Reserve Bank of Chicago, *Business Conditions*, August 1975, p. 15.

3 In this way favoritism to housing has facilitated purchases of consumer durables, according to Rudolph G. Penner, "Taxation and the Allocation of Credit," in *Studies*, ed. Kaminow and O'Brien, pp. 68-69.

4 Dwight M. Jaffee, "Housing Finance and Mortgage Market Policy," in Karl Brunner et al., *Government Credit Allocation* (San Francisco: Institute for Contemporary Studies, 1975), pp. 108-9, quotation from p. 109.

the form of financing without much affecting the number of houses built. More generally, Meltzer found no evidence that the availability of a particular type of credit has any important or lasting effects on what kinds of assets individuals acquire.[5] As he and Francisco Arcelus concluded in an earlier study,

> Financial variables have very little lasting effect on real variables. Houses are no different in this respect than other assets. The supply and demand functions depend on relative prices, wealth or income, anticipations, tastes and productive opportunities, not on the amount of credit made available in one form or another. . . . The form in which credit is granted is far less important than is commonly believed.[6]

Large firms and wealthy individuals have obvious advantages in exploiting the fungibility of money and credit. For this reason, controls can have a quite unintended selective impact.[7] In this respect, credit controls bear an analogy with exchange controls. Rationing foreign exchange in favor of supposed high-priority purposes does the opposite of burdening the big operator for the sake of the little man. The difficulty of distinguishing between business trips and pleasure trips abroad suggests just one of the reasons why. Exchange controls and credit controls alike put a premium on having "contacts" and engaging in far-flung and diversified activities. Credit controls also favor, relatively, borrowers with enough size, information, and influence to divert their credit demands to unregulated markets.

---

[5] "Credit Availability and Economic Decisions: Some Evidence from the Mortgage and Housing Markets," *Journal of Finance*, vol. 29 (June 1974), pp. 763-77, reprinted in Brunner et al., *Government Credit Allocation*, pp. 123-50. A summary by Karl Brunner appears on pp. 9-10.

[6] Francisco Arcelus and Allan Meltzer, "The Markets for Housing and Housing Services," *Journal of Money, Credit and Banking*, vol. 5 (February 1973), p. 95. The authors estimated demand equations for housing services and for new houses, using the stock of mortgage credit as one of the explanatory variables. Housing demand turned out to be related negatively to mortgage credit, other variables remaining unchanged. "There is no plausible interpretation of these findings . . . that is consistent with the standard . . . emphasis given to mortgage credit as a determinant of demand" (p. 86). Combined with other calculations, these results led Arcelus and Meltzer to "the conclusion that the effect of mortgage credit on housing is small and insignificant" (p. 95).

[7] As Milton Friedman has said of consumer credit controls, they impose the heaviest burden on people who have the fewest or poorest alternatives to buying on the prohibited terms. In effect they subsidize people who would in any case buy for cash. Friedman in *Money and Economic Activity*, ed. Lawrence S. Ritter, 2nd ed. (Boston: Houghton Mifflin, 1961), selection #28.

Just as selective controls may affect more the labeling than the amounts of credit extended to individual borrowers, so it may have only trivial effects on commercial banks' borrowing from the central bank. This remark refers in particular to preferential rediscounting, that is, especially favorable terms on central-bank loans to commercial banks using bank loans of officially favored types for collateral. The commercial banks may simply respond by rediscounting more of their favored and less of their nonfavored loans, leaving the pattern of their own lending pretty much unchanged.[8]

Circumvention through the Market

So far we have been considering evasion of controls by individual borrowers or lenders. But circumvention can also work indirectly, through market channels, and even without anyone's deliberately trying to evade the controls. (It can also work, as we shall see presently, through changes in financial institutions and practices.) Suppose that government agencies float bond issues and either relend the proceeds to savings institutions specializing in home finance or buy mortgages directly. By meeting the demands of creditworthy mortgage borrowers and lowering mortgage interest rates, these actions make mortgage loans less attractive to private lenders who therefore channel their own funds elsewhere. Also, if an agency steps up its buying of housing mortgages, it will have to raise more funds itself. It may sell securities to a pension fund that would otherwise have bought corporate bonds. Instead of the bonds, the corporation in question might then issue commercial paper, which banks may buy instead of mortgages that they would otherwise have bought.[9]

---

[8] Omotunde E. G. Johnson, "Direct Credit Controls in a Development Context: The Case of African Countries," in Brunner et al., *Government Credit Allocation*, p. 168.

[9] This last example is due to Jack M. Guttentag, "Selective Credit Controls on Residential Mortgage Credit," in *Studies*, ed. Kaminow and O'Brien, pp. 56-57 and footnotes. Sidney S. Hicks has developed analysis and tentative evidence suggesting that when government-owned and government-sponsored agencies in the United States borrow funds to rechannel them into housing, the induced rise in open-market interest rates leads to disintermediation out of savings and loan associations, a reduction in the total supply of mortgage loans and a rise in mortgage interest rates, and thus a restraint on housing starts. In addition, the activities of the federal agencies appear to have intensified the instability of housing construction. "Disintermediation, Government Agencies, and Housing: Is the Cure Worse than the Disease?" (manuscript, Florida State Univer-

In the capital markets, competition of government agencies with other borrowers will tend to raise interest rates. In response, private lenders will to some extent make mortgage loans indirectly, through these agencies, that they would otherwise have made directly. The more sensitively lenders can adjust their portfolios to differences in interest rates in different sectors of the credit and capital markets, the smaller would those relative interest-rate movements be. Given high substitutability among assets in lenders' portfolios, the government could be doing less to change the amounts of funds going into various uses than to change the detailed channeling and the labeling of those funds.

For another example of circumvention through the market, suppose that the government sets differential reserve requirements on different types of bank loan—a low requirement (or even a reserve credit) on mortgage loans and a high requirement on consumer loans. Banks would no doubt respond by shifting the pattern of their lending. The resulting decline of interest rates on mortgages and rise of rates on consumer loans would give other lenders—perhaps life-insurance companies or pension funds—incentives to make fewer mortgage loans and to channel more of their funds, perhaps indirectly, into consumer credit.[10] To put the point more generally, controls that succeed in making regulated institutions shift their funds in governmentally favored directions will depress interest yields on the favored classes of loans and investments and raise them on others. Uncontrolled lenders will then shift their lending away from the favored classes. Borrowers displaced at the controlled institutions, meanwhile, will bid up interest rates and attract funds from other lenders or on the open market.[11] The more sensitively uncontrolled lenders respond to the interest-rate tendencies caused by the initial controls, the less effective will those controls be (and the

sity, October 1976). If Hick's evidence is correct, she has provided a new example of Brozen's Law (so called for Professor Yale Brozen): "Most obviously *true* economic policy propositions are false."

Sanford Rose reviews evidence (assembled by Professor Dwight Jaffee in particular) suggesting that when the federal agencies buy mortgages, they drive down yields, causing other mortgage lenders, such as commercial banks and life insurance companies, to shift into more attractive assets, including bonds of the housing agencies themselves. "Why Fannie, Ginnie, and Freddy Can't Do It," *Fortune*, March 1977, esp. pp. 111, 113.

[10] Lawrence S. Ritter and William L. Silber, *Principles of Money, Banking, and Financial Markets* (New York: Basic Books, 1974), pp. 418-19.

[11] Federal Reserve Chairman Arthur Burns in U.S., Congress, *Hearings*, p. 207. Burns was discussing, in particular, the idea of applying asset reserve supplements and credits to banks belonging to the Federal Reserve System.

smaller the actual interest-rate movements). It is unlikely, in fact, that production of particular goods will depend strongly on the terms or availability of loans solely from the sources that their buyers traditionally rely on.

Advocacy of selective credit policies apparently rests not only on unsupported beliefs about how mortgage programs have stimulated housing but also on the impression that controls on consumer credit during and after World War II did restrain spending on consumer durable goods.[12] Conditions of over a quarter-century ago were relatively favorable to the apparent success of consumer credit controls. Fewer financial channels existed then than now; in particular, consumers did not use revolving credit and credit cards. The controls were in effect for only a few years, so the full effects of learning how to beat the system, partly through changes in credit institutions and practices, did not have a chance to show themselves. A key factor restraining purchases of consumer durable goods must have been their sheer unavailability because of withdrawal of men and materials into war production. More generally, consumer credit must be one of the relatively controllable types of credit, since individuals, as consumers, generally engage in smaller and less diverse transactions than do business firms; they have fewer alternative sources of financing. Thus, the consumer durable-goods sector during the 1940s and early 1950s afforded a relatively favorable test of whether selective credit controls can work.[13]

Even so, and even specifically for the period after the end of wartime shortages, the evidence is far from persuasive. Hamburger and Zwick ran simple correlations between total spending on consumer durable goods and changes in the outstanding stock of installment credit. Alternatively, they used extensions of installment credit as the explanatory variable. They also ran correlations between expenditures on automobiles in particular and changes in the outstanding stock of automobile installment credit (and, alternatively, extensions of such credit). The correlations turned out fairly strong for the entire period from the first quarter of 1948 through the first quarter of 1975, but much weaker for the subperiod from the first quarter of 1948 through the fourth quarter of 1952, during two parts

---

[12] Michael J. Hamburger and Burton Zwick, "The Effect of Installment Credit Controls on Consumer Expenditures and the Allocation of Real Resources" (typescript, Federal Reserve Bank of New York, 1974-1975), p. 31.

[13] Most of these points appear also in Paul Smith, "A Review of the Theoretical and Administrative History of Consumer Credit Controls," in Studies, ed. Kaminow and O'Brien, pp. 138ff., and Ira P. Kaminow, "Discussion," in FRBB, Techniques, pp. 60-61.

of which controls were in effect. This breakdown of the relation between expenditure and installment credit suggests to Hamburger and Zwick that consumers were able to maintain their spending patterns either by resort to alternative types of credit or by drawing on their savings.

Hamburger and Zwick also ran multiple regressions for the determinants of spending on automobiles and other consumer durables and the amount of spending on each. In both, the average values of the errors for the quarter-years in which installment credit controls were in effect turned out quite similar to the average errors for the quarters without controls. In both the automobile equation and the equation for other durables, introducing a dummy variable for controls-on or controls-off during each quarter-year of the 1948–1952 period left the coefficients of the other explanatory variables practically unchanged; and the dummy's coefficient had only a low degree of statistical significance. The authors saw these further results as indicating that controls did not affect expenditures on automobiles and other consumer durables during 1948–1952.

To check their results further, Hamburger and Zwick analyzed the portfolio behavior of individuals, firms, and financial institutions to identify how borrowers and lenders responded to controls. One of several possibilities is that individuals and firms with access to credit might buy durable goods and lease them to others to whom credit had been reduced. Evidence gathered in the New York Federal Reserve District suggests that banks extend (and borrowers use) unsecured personal loans in place of installment loans when the latter are subject to control.[14] Borrowers and financial markets and institutions have become more sophisticated since the period of controls described above. That fact, along with evidence on the flexible response of lender portfolios to asset restrictions, led the authors "to believe that the capacity to alter real resource allocation through selective credit policies in today's economy is unlikely to be greater, and may well be less, than during the 1948–52 period of controls on installment credit."[15] While no single piece of their evidence is conclusive, the authors maintain that its cumulative effect does shift the burden of proof from those who think that controls leave the

---

[14] Automobile dealers used to exploit another loophole to get around controls. A dealer would inflate both the trade-in value of his customer's old car and the new car's price to make the trade-in cover the required down payment. Over time, "lenders could develop similar schemes that would largely eliminate the effect of a credit allocations system." Thomas Mayer, "The Case against Credit Allocations," *National Review*, December 19, 1975, p. 1472.

[15] Hamburger and Zwick, "Installment Credit Controls," esp. pp. 30–31, 33.

composition of expenditures unaffected onto those who think otherwise.[16]

The Costs of Circumvention

Selective credit controls and their circumvention have costs. Some take the form of reduced financial efficiency, greater instability of financial institutions, and proliferation of controls in efforts to plug loopholes. The distinction between circumvention and its consequences is, of course, unavoidably fuzzy.

Controls covering only some of the channels of financial intermediation cause more credit to flow through unregulated channels or new channels.[17] Firms hampered in borrowing from financial institutions may resort to trade credit: they increase their borrowing from supplier firms by paying less promptly for merchandise bought. Their suppliers can in effect collect interest by charging higher prices, as when their customers no longer qualify for prompt-payment discounts. Thus compensated, the firms selling on credit are better able to bid for credit from financial institutions, which, if restricted in lending to certain types of firm or for certain purposes, will have more loanable funds for other borrowers or purposes. Firms supplying increased trade credit in effect take on financial intermediation as a sideline to their regular business. Selective controls, as an observer of the Italian scene has noted, can leave the distribution of credit among final users unchanged. Statistical documentation of this point is difficult to obtain, which in itself carries implications about the workability of controls. Multiplication of incentives for getting around them makes it all the more difficult for the authorities to learn, let alone to regulate, what is occurring.[18] When unable to accommodate their business customers, banks often informally help them arrange direct loans from firms having surplus

---

[16] The authors comment on earlier studies purporting to reach conclusions contrary to their own. They point out that correlations between particular types of expenditure and types of credit do not establish the direction of causation, and they explain the superiority of their own over alternative equations including a controls-on-or-off dummy variable. See their pages 17-18, 20, 24-25 in particular.

[17] This tendency has been unmistakable in foreign countries. Donald R. Hodgman, *Selective Credit Controls in Western Europe* (Chicago: Association of Reserve City Bankers, 1976), esp. p. 70.

[18] Tommaso Padoa-Schioppa, "Selective Credit Policy: Italy's Recent Experience," Banca Nationale del Lavoro *Quarterly Review*, no. 112 (March 1975), p. 48.

funds, sometimes adding their own guarantees. Large firms may obtain credit abroad if denied it at home. All such substitutions suggest that less efficient but unregulated channels of credit can expand at the expense of more efficient but regulated ones.[19]

Regulating particular financial institutions or channels weakens them in relation to others. For example, the government has tried to increase the demand for mortgages by restricting the portfolios of savings and loan associations and mutual savings banks to mortgages and various government and agency securities. Asset reserve requirements, if instituted, would have qualitatively similar effects. The regulated institutions would acquire portfolios with different combinations of risk and yield on their assets than they would freely choose. Their position would be much the same as if they suffered from discriminatory taxation. Impairment of their earning power would also impair their ability to compete for deposits. They would tend to shrivel relative to less tightly regulated institutions and relative to new channels of lending.

To offset the damage done to the savings institutions, supposedly remedial measures were adopted, including tax advantages and deposit-interest ceilings to restrain competition from commercial banks. Restrictions introduced over the period 1966–1970 on interest-rate competition among deposit institutions were bypassed in new ways, including the further evolution of the commercial-paper market and of real estate investment trusts (the latter not being a notably stable component of the financial system). Controls over foreign lending, as well as deposit-interest ceilings, spurred the growth of the Eurodollar market, which some observers consider a potential source of instability. Money-market mutual funds were invented in the early 1970s. Several of them offer checking privileges, which may confuse the definition of money and make it harder for the Federal Reserve to follow a correct policy.[20]

Consequences like these might aptly be called "institutional instability"; less tightly regulated institutions flourish or are invented. Partly because of institutional instability, apparent success of selective credit controls in the short run is unlikely to endure in the long run.

"Participants in financial markets are very creative when it comes to circumventing regulations." Any initial success of new controls

---

[19] Hodgman, *Western Europe*, p. 70.

[20] Maurice Mann and Harris C. Friedman, "Controlling Lender Behavior: Asset and Liability Restraints," in FRBB, *Techniques*, p. 37; Merris, "Credit Allocation," pp. 16-17; Penner, "Taxation," p. 92; Fortune, "Discussion," in FRBB, *Techniques*, p. 46; and Mayer, "Financial Guidelines," pp. 88-89.

spurs this creativeness. If consumers cannot get bank credit for buying automobiles because, say, banks are investing heavily in sewer bonds, then the car dealers will arrange the necessary financing. Probably they will work with the car manufacturers, who can float bonds and use the proceeds for any desired purpose, including loans to customers.[21]

Some possibilities of circumvention suggest that controls might be more effective if applied to borrowers rather than to lenders alone. To be effective, lender-oriented controls must affect the asset choices of individuals, commercial banks, thrift institutions, life-insurance companies, pension funds, firms engaged in financial intermediation as a sideline, and other lenders engaged, as a group, in lending and investing in practically all sectors of the economy and for practically all purposes. It might be administratively simpler to concentrate restrictions on a relatively few types of nonpreferred borrower. These are widely supposed to be consumers (borrowing for purposes other than housing) and, in particular, large corporations.[22]

Counting against this idea are the much larger number of borrowers than of lending institutions and the problems of monitoring borrowers to see that they do not divert borrowed funds to relatively disfavored purposes. Intended discrimination among borrowers could be defeated to the extent that favored borrowers obtain funds on behalf of others. Many state and local governments, for example, try to attract business firms into their jurisdictions by constructing factories and other facilities with funds obtained by floating their own tax-exempt bonds. The Interest Equalization Tax provides an example of circumvention in a more roundabout way. The tax made the U.S. capital markets less attractive than otherwise for European borrowers, who therefore competed more eagerly to borrow from fellow Europeans, including ones who would otherwise have invested in the United States. To that extent, the tax merely reduced gross inflows and outflows of funds and the role of U.S. financial institutions as intermediaries between European lenders and European borrowers instead of straightforwardly reducing the net outflow of funds from the United States.

These considerations lead to the conjecture that measures discriminating for or against the debt of particular classes of borrow-

---

21 Ritter and Silber, *Principles of Money, Banking*, p. 419.

22 Fortune, "Discussion," in FRBB, *Techniques*, pp. 46-47, and Guttentag, "Mortgage Credit," pp. 57-58. The suggestions reported here again call to mind the distinction between negative and positive controls (see chapter 1, under "Precedents") and the question of which type is likely to be more effective.

ers are likely to work more effectively than measures to promote or restrict credit for particular purposes. (Multiactivity borrowers can defeat the latter kind of discrimination, as we have already noted, by the internal juggling of fungible funds.) On the other hand, discrimination among classes of issuers of obligations is not exactly what advocates of selective credit controls typically want; they want discrimination among end-uses of credit. Whether that kind of discrimination can be circumvented is the question that really concerns us here, and not how easily people might avoid various less ambitious control measures.

Loopholes and the Proliferation of Controls

On this main question, we must conclude that limited regulation of only certain types of lending institution would do little to redirect credit into favored directions. Because of several conditions—the fungibility of money and credit, the wide variety of existing financial institutions and the flexibility of the portfolios of at least some of them, the demonstrated possibilities of introducing new financial institutions and practices, and, in general, the wide range of financial channels actually and potentially open to borrowers and lenders alike—blocking particular channels of credit would only cause others to expand. Circumvention would become all the more nearly complete as time went on. If credit controls were to have a significant and durable influence on the allocation of real resources, they would have to be comprehensive. They would have to cover all types of financial institution, including new types whenever they appeared, all markets for debt and equity securities, the entire network of trade credit, and all international borrowing, lending, and investing. Control over the actual end-uses of credit would require detailed regulation of almost every facet of the economy.[23] To forestall all circumvention, the authorities would have to insist on everyone's obtaining advance permission to do practically anything financial. Job opportunities for controllers would abound.

The argument that controls would have to be comprehensive to be effective is widely accepted even by advocates of controls, some of whom, one suspects, even welcome its truth. Lester Thurow, who has called for applying asset reserve requirements to financial institutions, frankly doubts

---

[23] See Beryl F. Sprinkel, p. 157, and Arthur Burns, p. 204, in U.S., Congress, *Hearings*, and Merris, "Credit Allocation," p. 18.

that you can compartmentalize financial intermediaries so that institutions that are under different regulatory handicaps do not compete with each other. . . . There probably is no set of regulations that could stop poaching on the other guy's turf. As a result, all regulations should be across-the-board regulations on all intermediaries.

All would be required to take part, for example, in housing finance. This does not mean, however, that every institution would have to make housing loans at the retail level. "Specialized housing institutions could issue bonds for those institutions with no expertise in housing and no desire to get into this business." [24]

Even so, Thurow's recommendations do not answer all questions; nor would implementing them thwart all circumvention. Does Thurow really mean that *all* financial institutions would have to hold housing paper? What about mutual funds and pension funds intended specifically for investment in stocks? What about independent finance companies and financing subsidiaries of manufacturing corporations? What about corporations extending trade credit without use of subsidiaries? Would investment bankers have to make sure that specified fractions of the stocks and bonds they were underwriting were being issued to raise funds for the favored purposes? And even if all these institutions, and more, were brought under the controls, what would be done about the sale of new stock and bond issues by corporations directly to savers? After all, as controls burdened the channels of financial intermediation more and more heavily, interest-rate incentives would grow stronger for direct transactions between security-issuers and savers.[25]

Interferences with the working of financial markets would push business firms into increased reliance on the plowback of earnings into the business. Yet critics of financial freedom of choice (including Thurow) typically voice suspicions of internal finance. A system of controls leading (however unintentionally) to heavy reliance on internal finance would discriminate relatively in favor of established business firms and against new or struggling firms. It would also discriminate against nonbusiness borrowers, who would be less likely than business firms to have available retained earnings and depreciation funds.

The history of margin requirements on credit for stock purchases in the United States illustrates the need to extend controls

---

[24] Lester Thurow, "Proposals for Rechanneling Funds to Meet Social Priorities," in FRBB, *Policies*, pp. 179, 186-87.

[25] Eli Shapiro raises these questions about Thurow's proposals in FRBB, *Policies*, pp. 202-3.

further and further as borrowers and lenders contrive loopholes. At first, in 1934, the requirement covered only loans from brokers and dealers to customers for buying or carrying stocks. As early as 1936 the controls were extended to banks. In 1958, when at least 90 percent cash was required for stock purchases, the *Wall Street Journal* listed numerous ways of evading the requirement: acquiring "rights" to new stock issues through brokerage firms; swapping convertible bonds for stock; borrowing from banks on securities on the false assurance that the proceeds would not be used to buy stock; pledging other possessions, such as life insurance, to raise money for buying stocks; and obtaining credit by placing orders for stock through foreign brokers. As a senior partner of a New York Stock Exchange member firm said, "With margin requirements tighter, it's only human nature that some people will be looking for angles." In 1959 the *Journal* illustrated the metaphysics that the Federal Reserve had to get into as it discussed the board's proposals for clarifying what loans collateralized by stock would and what ones would not be considered loans for the purpose of "carrying" stock. A loan would be deemed for that purpose "if the borrower owns any registered stock, whether or not he has pledged it as security for the loan, which he has not owned free of any lien for as much as one year." In 1968 margin requirements were extended to bonds convertible into stocks and to all domestic lenders having securities lending as an important part of their business. In 1970 the requirements were extended to cover credit provided to U.S. borrowers by foreign lending institutions on the grounds that those lenders tended to obtain financing, in turn, from U.S. sources.[26]

Experience with margin requirements is, if anything, a fairly easy test of selective controls, for their aim is merely to remedy a supposed disorder in a particular financial market. The question does not arise of real resource allocation escaping an intended effect. If combatting circumvention even of margin requirements requires repeated extension of their coverage, that fact does not speak well for selective controls with more ambitious purposes.

Margin requirements are not the only example. The Federal Reserve has met failure time and again, as Edward J. Kane reminds us, with other detailed interventions in specific markets. The real-bills discounting policy of its early years, its real estate and

---

[26] Thomas D. Simpson, *Money, Banking, and Economic Analysis* (Englewood Cliffs, N.J.: Prentice-Hall, 1976), p. 237; Lester V. Chandler, *The Economics of Money and Banking*, 6th ed. (New York: Harper & Row, 1973), p. 264; Thomas E. Van Dahm, *Money and Banking* (Lexington, Mass.: Heath, 1975), p. 489; and *Wall Street Journal*, October 21, 1958, p. 30, and December 10, 1959, p. 15.

consumer-credit controls, and notable attempts at "moral suasion" all miscarried. Efforts to enforce deposit-interest ceilings involved stopgap measures that in turn bred further measures until the control system partially broke down (on large certificates of deposit). To plug loopholes, new restrictions were introduced on Eurodollars, federal funds, commercial paper, and Treasury bills. Banks and nonfinancial corporations issued instruments competing with U.S. savings bonds. When open-market interest rates fell below deposit-interest ceilings, new problems appeared. The staff of the Federal Reserve was no match for the private economy, where firms had to find loopholes to survive. Private institutions were able to out-maneuver the Federal Reserve because, on balance, they recruit more talented people, train and motivate and pay them better, and drive them harder when the going gets tough. Managers and employees of private firms outnumber their counterparts at the Federal Reserve and personally have more at stake.[27]

Because it works partly through development of new financial institutions and practices, circumvention of controls can be more nearly complete in the long run than in the short run. A learning factor is at work. As Hodgman said of the United Kingdom in the 1960s, the longer controls remained in effect, the more the uncon-trolled channels of financial intermediation expanded at the expense of the controlled ones. Acceptance houses and foreign and overseas banks gained ground on the clearing banks. The banks organized finance-house subsidiaries to compete for higher-interest-bearing and longer-maturity deposits than cartel understandings sanctioned. Markets for interbank deposits, sterling certificates of deposit, and local-authority deposits challenged the controlled traditional money market. The authorities had to keep broadening their efforts as they raced to cope with uncontrolled flows of credit.[28]

Like new versus old ones, so unanticipated controls are likely to have more of an impact than expected ones. (This is not necessarily a good thing. Householders can cope better with pre-announced interruptions of electricity or water than with unexpected interruptions. Similarly, the short-run effectiveness of surprise controls may be bought at the expense of financial disruptions and bankruptcies, whereas responses to anticipated or old and familiar controls could stretch out more smoothly over time.) [29]

---

[27] Edward J. Kane, "Discussion," in FRBB, *Policies*, pp. 196-97.

[28] Donald R. Hodgman, "Credit Controls in Western Europe: An Evaluative Review," in FRBB, *Techniques*, p. 146.

[29] See Wood, "Large Firms," in *Studies*, ed. Kaminow and O'Brien, pp. 148ff.

The changing effectiveness of controls over time or according to whether they are expected or a surprise has several implications. Supposed econometric evidence on the contrasting behavior of an economy when controls were "on" and when they were "off" tells little about enduring effectiveness. Switching controls on and off, or altering them, can bring perverse results if the controllers cannot predict how fast their effects will come and how long they will last. Unless the controllers have sound knowledge of such matters as the time path of responses to alterations in the controls, those alterations can produce uncertainty and potentially destabilizing effects.[30] Controls will have to be changed from time to time in direction, intensity, and nature, partly to cope with newly developed methods of circumventing them. Yet success in wielding controls flexibly puts great demands on the knowledge and predictive power of the authorities.

Further Costs

Costs mount as authorities try to enforce controls, as private parties discover loopholes and devise new credit institutions and practices, and as the authorities extend the controls in response. Controls on financial intermediaries work much like a tax on them, lowering effective interest rates to savers and raising them to borrowers.[31] The administrative costs and problems include the need for detailed data and elaborate bookkeeping for monitoring millions of individual loans.[32] Managers have to be trained and other start-up costs borne for new institutions, and customers have to take the time and trouble to learn about them.[33] The controls, and responses to them, artificially hasten the obsolescence of knowledge and impose the costs of keeping abreast of the artificially changing scene. Real resources are diverted from productive employments.

A broader cost, especially as controls effectively limit the scale of business of individual institutions and types of institution, is interference with competition. Controls shelter less efficient lenders

---

[30] John Lintner, "Do We Know Enough to Adopt a Variable Investment Tax Credit?" in FRBB, *Techniques*, esp. p. 115, where Lintner is referring to a variable investment tax credit in particular.

[31] This, says Omotunde Johnson, is probably the greatest welfare cost of controls in less-developed countries. "Development Context," p. 173.

[32] Arthur Burns in U.S., Congress, *Hearings*, p. 207.

[33] Mayer, "Financial Guidelines," p. 88.

from expansion by their more efficient rivals. They impede constructive innovation [34]—for not all the innovation they stimulate is constructive from the social point of view. The Bank of France has cited as the most serious consequence of credit ceilings that they freeze competition by subjecting the activity of all credit establishments to common norms.[35] An analogy from the theory of international trade policy comes to mind—the anticompetitive effects of import quotas.

Controls in support of a low-interest-rate policy may depress domestic saving and encourage capital outflow, prompting resort to exchange control with all of its problems, including possible retaliation. Controls may interfere with noninflationary management of the money supply.[36] A scheme of supplementary reserve requirements and reserve credits would make more data essential to the money managers. Data on volumes of supplementary reserves would have to be collected every week and perhaps even every day, as is now done for demand deposits.[37] Differential reserve requirements against assets would further loosen the link between bank reserves and measures of the money supply. Every shift of bank loans and investments between priority and nonpriority categories would alter the total volume of bank deposits that the existing volume of bank reserves could support and so would make total bank assets and deposits either shrink or expand. Since the Federal Reserve could hardly predict changes in the composition of bank assets from one reserve period to the next, it would meet greater difficulty than it already does in judging how much to add to total reserves to achieve any desired growth rate in the monetary aggregates.[38]

---

[34] Donald R. Hodgman, *National Monetary Policies and International Monetary Cooperation* (Boston: Little, Brown, 1974), p. 218, and Hodgman, *Western Europe*, p. 70.

[35] Quoted in Hodgman, *Western Europe*, p. 27. Compare David A. Alhadeff, *Competition and Controls in Banking* (Berkeley and Los Angeles: University of California Press, 1968), p. 154: "In an unregulated *competitive* market, competition spurs each firm to increase its efficiency. As the French authorities undermined this market spur to greater bank efficiency by restraining bank competition, they have employed various administrative measures to compensate at least in part for the weakened market pressures." Alhadeff goes on to mention research undertaken by the Conseil National du Crédit into rationalizing bank operations and otherwise cutting costs.

[36] See chapter 1, under "Support of Macro Policy," chapter 2, under "The Costs of Circumvention," and Hodgman, *National Monetary Policies*, p. 218.

[37] Merris, "Credit Allocation," p. 18.

[38] Federal Reserve Chairman Arthur Burns in U.S., Congress, *Hearings*, pp. 206-7.

Arbitrariness and unfairness also count among the costs of controls. As controls become more comprehensive and complex, the authorities are less able to base their decisions and actions on objective economic and market criteria. Bureaucratic rules become all the more essential and decisions based on incomplete information all the more unavoidable. Systems of controls that multiply categories entitled to special treatment become vulnerable to the pleading of special interests. Guidelines at odds with normal business practices and profit criteria are weak and ineffective. A serious attempt at effectiveness would entail setting goals for individual credit institutions, checking compliance frequently and thoroughly, and imposing real penalties.[39] What should the dollar volumes of credit be in each favored and disfavored category for each type of financial institution? What should the percentage requirements be for supplementary reserves and reserve credits? Quantifying such requirements and varying them as business conditions changed would pose thorny problems.[40]

The complexity of detailed monitoring and enforcement suggests appealing for voluntary compliance, compliance with the spirit and not just the letter of the regulations. Whether compliance is avowedly voluntary or ease of evasion makes compliance voluntary in effect, such an approach tends to penalize the good guys who do comply to the advantage of the bad guys who do not. Expecting people to act against their own economic interest tends to undercut the signaling function of prices and the incentive of loss-avoidance and profit; with its signals and incentives impaired, the price mechanism becomes less effective in organizing economic activity to produce preferred goods and services and to produce them efficiently. How are people to know, then, when it is proper and when improper to pursue economic gain? To exhort people to think of compliance as in their own interest when it plainly is not, or to call for self-sacrifice as if it were the essence of morality, is to undercut the rational basis of morality and even undercut rationality itself. A kind of perverse selection results. This point is similar to Garrett Hardin's point about the voluntary approach to population control in an overpopulated country: the people who comply contribute to the population relatively few persons exposed in their formative years to their own moral standards (and also inheriting whatever genes may be relevant). The noncompliers will have

---

[39] Hodgman, *Western Europe*, p. 69, and Hodgman, "Selective Credit Controls," pp. 335-36.

[40] Merris, "Credit Allocation," p. 18.

relatively many children, who will grow up exposed to the lower moral standards of their parents (as well as having any relevant "bad" genes). Over time, these others will outbreed the decent people.[41] In economic affairs, similarly, compliant borrowers and lenders who abide by the spirit of the regulations will, by that very token, sacrifice opportunities to those who are less public-spirited or less gullible. (Compare public-spirited car owners who heed appeals for restraint in driving. By doing so, they leave more gasoline available, and at a lower price than otherwise, to drivers less public-spirited than themselves.) Eventually such effects become evident, further supporting the perverse idea that morality is for suckers and dupes.

In contrast with voluntary controls or easily evaded ones, legally enacted and actually enforceable penalties for violations do tend to make compliance serve the individual's self-interest. This is an argument for trying to keep laws simple, understandable, in conformity with deep-seated notions of right and wrong, and actually enforceable.[42] Economic regulations of the opposite character tend to work unfairness and undermine morality.

A similarly broad cost is that selective credit controls tend to undercut the profit orientation and market character of financial markets and of the whole economic system. They nudge the economy in the direction of central planning. This issue is discussed further toward the end of this study.[43]

Although the costs of circumventing controls should to some extent deter the officially disfavored uses of credit, the costs will not fall squarely on those uses. Instead, the costs of circumvention, enforcement, and loophole-plugging, and the broader costs just mentioned, will spread through the economic system generally. They will ultimately burden officially favored as well as disfavored activities.

[41] Garrett Hardin, "The Tragedy of the Commons," reprinted from *Science*, vol. 162 (1968), pp. 1243-48, in *Population, Evolution, and Birth Control*, ed. Garrett Hardin, 2nd ed. (San Francisco: Freeman, 1969), pp. 367-81. I cite Hardin only to clarify the point, not to echo his recommendation on an issue remote from the present topic.

[42] For further development of these themes, see my "Economics and Principles," *Southern Economic Journal*, vol. 42 (April 1976), pp. 559-71. As explained there, not all reliance on people's voluntary decency is wrong. Precisely because the willingness to behave decently is a scarce resource, it is a shame to waste and strain it by economic controls that create unnecessary tensions between decency and rational self-interest.

[43] See chapter 3.

Experience Abroad

No doubt a comprehensive and detailed system of controls wielded by a sufficiently extensive administrative apparatus could influence the allocations of credit and real resources. The authorities are more likely to achieve their purposes if private parties have less scope to evade the regulations through domestic and international channels. Conditions tending to keep this scope narrow include high concentration in banking, government ownership of banks and other key intermediaries and investment funds, limited variety and clear-cut specialization among credit institutions, controls covering substantially all types of credit institution, restrictions on access to the money market, official control over new security issues, exchange controls, and reinforcement by tax and subsidy measures.[44]

All these preconditions limit the lessons to be drawn from experience with credit controls in other countries. Any supposedly successful foreign experience—something we will have to look at further—says little in favor of introducing the controls in the United States. Here, the institutional context is different. The capital and credit markets, like the entire economy, are larger and more diversified, less concentrated, and generally more competitive, and, up to now, less tightly regulated. In addition, financial regulations are less fully buttressed by other policy measures.

Reviewing foreign experience with selective controls in the early years after World War II, Peter Fousek found that central banks, generally speaking, seem not to have obtained the results they sought except when the selective controls were buttressed with effective general controls over quantities of money and credit. Elaborate systems of selective controls proved disappointing. Country after country either abandoned them or readapted them as an adjunct to general quantitative controls. Fousek found selective controls most effective where money and capital markets were rudimentary, as in underdeveloped countries, where institutional obstacles delayed the impact of general credit controls on certain economic sectors, or where fluctuations in general demand had been concentrated in certain well-defined sectors sensitive to the supply of credit. "The hazard, as the foreign experience shows, lies in any attempt to use selective or direct controls over credit as a substitute for general controls."[45]

---

[44] Hodgman, "Selective Credit Controls," pp. 355-56, and *National Monetary Policies*, pp. 204-5, where Hodgman then goes on to examine these favorable factors in detail.

[45] Peter G. Fousek, *Foreign Central Banking: The Instruments of Monetary*

The United Kingdom. More recent foreign experience casts doubt, by and large, on whether controls have worked or can work satisfactorily.[46] In the United Kingdom, the postwar history of monetary policy up to 1971 featured escalation of administrative interventions into financial markets, leading to the progressive replacement of general monetary policy by selective controls.[47] During World War II, the authorities began to address "requests" to the banks, trying not only to regulate the volume of bank credit but also to favor certain uses over others. Particularly during the immediate postwar years, they emphasized credit to the export industries. The guidelines were usually phrased broadly, contradicting each other in some cases and leaving a good deal of detail to the interpretation and judgment of the banks. The entertainment industry, for example, was given low priority in its domestic aspect but high priority as a potential earner or saver of foreign exchange. Moral suasion sometimes had undesired side effects, undermining the effectiveness of other monetary controls. For example, when the authorities asked the banks to restrict their loans to installment-credit companies, those companies began soliciting deposits directly from the public, which contributed to the relative decline of the commercial banks. Where moral suasion did work as desired, special reasons could be cited. Bankers as well as the authorities had traditionally preferred informal methods to formal controls. Bankers well understood that legal sanctions could reinforce "requests" if necessary. The concentration of British banking in the hands of a few large branch-banking systems and the cartel-like character of banking aided communication. The banks recognized their common interests and the impact that each could have upon a proposed policy.[48]

Another British technique was to set a ceiling rate of expansion relative to a designated base period for total bank loans and to exempt priority categories from the ceilings, notably loans to export industries, shipbuilding, nationalized industries, and local authorities. The ceilings on loan expansion, set initially only for the clearing banks, were gradually extended to other institutions. By the late 1960s the Bank of England was sending information

---

Policy (New York: Federal Reserve Bank of New York, 1957), quotation from p. 81.

[46] First-hand research into this experience was beyond the scope of this work, but I have tried to canvass the best-known studies.

[47] Hodgman, *Western Europe*, p. 158.

[48] Alhadeff, *Competition*, pp. 315-17.

copies of its loan guidelines to associations of insurance companies, pension funds, building societies (equivalent to savings and loan associations), and commercial finance corporations.

Disadvantaged borrowers and lenders kept developing new channels of financial intermediation, provoking the authorities further to extend the scope and variety of direct regulations and to rely still less on market processes. According to an econometric study by Alan Pankratz, damming one channel of finance subsequently required attempting to dam several others. If credit ceilings were able to force any cutbacks in expenditures over the short run, the persons and firms affected were probably unsophisticated in financial affairs and relatively small and weak. Furthermore, the controls tended to protect established financial institutions from the competition of new and more efficient ones. Controls over short-term credit tended to shift the pressure of excess demand to the longer-term markets in the form of increased private issues of securities accompanied by reduced investor demand for government securities. As the Bank of England sought to hold down interest yields on government bonds in the face of deficit spending and sought to preserve a non-market-determined pattern of interest rates, it neglected money-supply restraint and so fed inflation.[49]

Increasing recognition of how poorly the old system had been working, together with the advent of a conservative government, led during 1971 to extensive reforms. These were meant to accord greater significance than before to the money supply, to put more reliance on price rather than nonprice rationing of credit, and to encourage competition in financial markets.[50] Policy did not, however, remain fully consistent with these objectives. Shortly after inaugurating the reforms, the government decided to "go for growth," hoping that expansion of money incomes would accelerate real economic growth without significantly raising prices. The money supply, measured broadly, was allowed to grow 25 percent in 1972. Some reversal of the financial disintermediation that had occurred under the earlier system, as well as continuing government budget deficits and use of a very broad definition of the money supply, obstructed firm monetary control. Tax provisions and other circumstances continued to make bank loans seem like bargains to corporate treasurers. The authorities remained willing to experiment with administrative regulation and even adopted an incomes policy late

---

[49] Hodgman, *National Monetary Policies*, pp. 184-87, and Hodgman, *Western Europe*, pp. 59-60, where Pankratz's study is quoted.

[50] Hodgman, *National Monetary Policies*, pp. 158-59, 190-96, and Hodgman, *Western Europe*, pp. 58-60.

in 1972 (following President Nixon's lead of a year before).[51] In short, backsliding from the new market-oriented policy ensued. Still, the dismal experience with the earlier system remains on record.

France. The French environment has been relatively favorable to selective controls. The commercial banking system is concentrated, and as early as 1945 the four principal commercial branch-banking systems were nationalized. The Caisse des Dépôts et Consignations (CDC) is the most important channel through which private savings reach the money and capital markets. It receives all funds deposited in state-owned and other savings banks and the liquid funds of the social security system. It finances housing and the construction projects of local governments and also lends to public and mixed-ownership industrial firms and other public credit institutions. Three public or semipublic financial institutions specialize in medium- and long-term credit. The so-called Treasury circuit embraces these three institutions and the CDC and more besides—the government budget, regional and local authorities, the social security system, the private and state savings banks that channel funds through the CDC, and the post office system of giro payments. The money and capital markets are highly regulated. Nonfinancial firms and individuals are excluded from direct participation in the money market, and nothing equivalent to a commercial-paper market exists. In connection with rediscounting, the Bank of France regularly reviews individual loans granted by commercial banks. Domestic controls are supplemented by controls over international capital movements.[52]

Under the system of credit allocation developed around 1946–1947, prior approval from the Bank of France was required for all credits to borrowers whose total credits, whether from one bank or many, exceeded a specified amount. Banks were instructed to screen all loan applications to determine not only whether the loan would be safe and profitable but also whether the funds could be obtained outside the banking system and whether they would be used for officially favored purposes. The government repeatedly issued instructions, requests, or recommendations that certain industries be favored and credit to others reduced.[53] Besides management of the flow of savings through the Treasury circuit and moral

---

[51] Marcus Miller, "Discussion," in FRBB, *Techniques*, pp. 176-77, and Hodgman, *Western Europe*, pp. 54, 60-63.

[52] Hodgman, *Western Europe*, p. 21.

[53] Alhadeff, *Competition*, pp. 208-10.

suasion of various types, the weapons wielded by the authorities include privileged rediscount categories at the Bank of France, requirements that banks hold minimum amounts of government securities and rediscountable medium-term credits, and exemption from ceiling rates of bank-credit expansion of loans for designated purposes. In short, French financial regulation is so comprehensive that it leaves relatively little chance of circumvention through alternative channels.[54]

Still, the system ran into problems. Detailed controls rather than interest rates rationed credit; in fact, a fallacious doctrine prevailed of holding down interest rates to hold down costs and prices. This approach, together with a variety of discounting privileges and exemptions from credit ceilings, undercut control of the money supply. Administrative controls contributed to rigidities and inefficiencies in financial organization and procedures. Growing awareness of these difficulties led the French authorities to begin experimenting in the late 1960s and early 1970s with reforms intended to place greater reliance on market forces.[55]

Belgium. In Belgium, also, the environment has been relatively favorable to using selective controls: state-controlled intermediaries form an important part of the financial system; the lending and borrowing activities of other credit institutions are controlled; the money-market is restricted; and exchange controls are in effect. "Thus, no important channel for credit remains outside the scope of supervision and control by the Belgian authorities."[56] Even so, it seems the authorities are not entirely happy with the results and consider selective credit controls as only temporary, emergency measures. Artificially holding down interest rates at a time of inflationary excess demand tended, according to the central bank, to stimulate spending decisions and the demand for credit. Credit ceilings had "the effect of encouraging the organization of new financing circuits operating outside the recognized financial intermediaries, perhaps with their cooperation." Fungibility came into play: "in many cases, as far as businesses are concerned, the 'selectivity' of the credits is lost in the unity of the cash holdings of the users of the funds."[57]

---

[54] Hodgman, *Western Europe*, pp. 25-26, and Hodgman, *National Monetary Policies*, p. 50.

[55] Hodgman, *National Monetary Policies*, esp. pp. 47-52, and Hodgman, *Western Europe*, pp. 22, 26-27.

[56] Hodgman, *Western Europe*, p. 15.

[57] National Bank of Belgium, *Report* for 1973, quoted in ibid., p. 15.

Italy. In Italy, the authorities have sought to influence credit allocation more than by indirectly controlling bank loans and terms to individual borrowers. Capital-market measures employed to favor high-priority investment activities include administrative screening of securities issues, investment grants or interest subsidies from the government budget, favorable loan terms from particular credit institutions, and permission given to banks to hold part of their obligatory reserves in the long-term securities of approved issuers. In Italy, as in France, the government gains leverage by owning banks and other credit institutions. The Italian money market has been regulated so that only the Treasury can be a net borrower and only financial institutions, principally banks, can use it for managing their liquidity positions.[58]

Possibilities of circumventing even the extensive Italian controls have not been lacking. Banks could transfer to special institutions their loans to enterprises subject to credit ceilings. Larger firms could withdraw trade credit from their smaller customers and suppliers, thus prodding these smaller firms to resort to direct bank loans; and large firms could borrow abroad, especially in the Euro-currency market.[59] Moreover, according to the governor of the Bank of Italy, qualitative control of bank credit is likely to have so many effects of opposite directions and unmeasurable intensity that the monetary authorities had best not attempt "the innumerable adjustments required by cyclical developments"; it would be safer "to leave these adjustments to the market process within the general conditions created by control of the volume of liquidity." [60]

A related complaint about Italian credit policies is that they have interfered with overall monetary policy. Bond-price pegging by the Bank of Italy has been an additional inflationary factor at times.[61]

Norway. In Norway the government has tried to hold interest rates below free-market levels and in particular to keep down interest rates paid by the government and the state investment banks, which in turn lend cheaply for housing, agriculture, hydroelectricity,

[58] Hodgman, *National Monetary Policies*, p. 108, and Hodgman, *Western Europe*, p. 30.

[59] Hodgman, *Western Europe*, pp. 36-37.

[60] *Annual Report*, 1973, p. 134, quoted in Hodgman, ibid., p. 35.

[61] Hodgman, *National Monetary Policies*, pp. 117-20, and James M. O'Brien, "Central Banking across the Atlantic: Another Dimension," Federal Reserve Bank of Philadelphia, *Business Review*, May 1975, p. 7.

and other officially favored purposes. At first the government sought to channel funds by negotiating agreements with banks and insurance companies regarding bond issues and credit; later it issued rules for compulsory purchases of bonds. Conditions are favorable to credit allocation by moral suasion in Norway in view of the small size and homogeneity of the population, the similar educational backgrounds of business and financial executives and government officials, and the resultant rapport and ease of communication.[62]

Even so, Norwegian credit allocation has shown questionable aspects. Informal persuasion has had to be implemented by tighter rules. Also, as Axel Dammann argues, when the government channels capital to preferred economic sectors at low cost without asking the national assembly to vote direct subsidies, it is bypassing the democratic process. The real cost of preferred projects is camouflaged, and comparison between them and other projects is hampered. Dammann argues that monetary measures are best suited for regulating general investment and savings conditions, while budgetary policy is better suited for bestowing favors and subsidies in a clear-cut and intelligible way.[63]

The Netherlands. In the Netherlands a selective influence on real resource allocation has not been the chief aim of credit controls. Instead, the authorities have tried to hold down interest rates generally and to bolster their macroeconomic policy against the difficulties associated with the openness of the Dutch economy to international trade and capital movements and (until early 1973) with the pegging of exchange rates. These expedients have not been notably successful in their macroeconomic purposes; and even so, circumvention has been evident. For example, banks responded to ceilings on short-term credit by lending at longer term; then they were asked to restrict their long-term lending also. Banks and brokers have helped customers to bypass bank credit ceilings by arranging direct loans from other bank customers, sometimes with bank guarantees of the borrowers' credit.[64]

---

[62] See Marvin M. Phaup, *The Nature of Modern Economic Planning: A Case Study of Norway* (Ph.D. diss., University of Virginia, 1966), esp. chapter 2.

[63] Axel Dammann, "Monetary Policy in Norway," in *Monetary Policy in Twelve Industrialized Countries*, ed. Karel Holbik (Boston: Federal Reserve Bank of Boston, 1973), esp. pp. 333-34, 369, 379.

[64] Hodgman, *National Monetary Policies*, pp. 143, 154-57, and Hodgman, *Western Europe*, p. 7.

Sweden. Sweden also provides examples of circumvention. Credit restrictions on banks and other lending institutions—and, in particular, ceilings on the growth of bank loans for purposes other than house building—brought rapid expansion of the credit market outside of those institutions. Instead of depositing their loanable funds in the banks, production firms began lending directly to each other. Some of these transactions took the form of trade credit, and some occurred over the borders of the country. This "gray market" resembles an incipient commercial-paper market. Large business firms are the chief lenders in it, thus taking on banking and credit-intermediation functions as a sideline, while business firms, municipalities, finance houses, and factors are the main borrowers. The commercial banks aided the market's development by putting borrowers and lenders in touch with each other and often by guaranteeing the credits arranged. Some banks have finance houses and factors as subsidiaries, permitting them to make certain kinds of loan without showing them on their balance sheets. As the gray market grew in importance in 1974, the authorities moved to impede its growth. Unhappy about losing the deposits of big business firms that were making direct loans instead, the commercial banks actually requested the Riksbank to take action.[65] This indicates no inconsistency on the part of the banks: each might want the gray market suppressed, yet, given its existence, make the best of it, helping their customers operate in it so as to retain their good will.

Macroeconomic Results. Besides bringing dubious microeconomic consequences, selective credit controls seem not to have improved macroeconomic results. Comparing data for the period 1961–1970 for Belgium, France, Italy, Sweden, and the United Kingdom, on the one hand, and Germany, the Netherlands, and the United States, on the other, James O'Brien concluded that countries substantially using credit controls for allocative purposes did not generally outperform other countries in growth of real output, restraint on price inflation, or lowness of interest rates.[66]

An Example of Success? The foregoing discussion is not meant to say that the foreign experience with selective credit controls has been a total and unequivocal failure. On the contrary, some success

[65] Assar Lindbeck, "Some Fiscal and Monetary Policy Experiments in Sweden," in FRBB, *Techniques*, p. 210, and Hodgman, *Western Europe*, p. 48.

[66] O'Brien, "Central Banking across the Atlantic," p. 9.

has been claimed, particularly in Sweden. Government debt has continued to be placed at relatively low and stable interest rates. The stock of dwellings has expanded rapidly since World War II, and cyclical variability in housing construction has been reduced.[67] Even so, the effects of credit controls on the mix of real investment are unclear. "Even over the longer haul, the proportion of investment devoted to housing in Sweden appears to be no greater than in the U.S." [68] Furthermore, "it now seems that the wrong type of housing was constructed. This arose because during the postwar housing shortage, individuals were satisfied with any housing that was produced. Now that shortages are eliminated, individuals are voicing their true preferences." [69]

The Swedish results, such as they are, must be seen in perspective. Sweden is a small country with a relatively homogeneous population and a relatively concentrated business and financial structure, including a system of a few large branch-banking systems. A closer approach to political consensus apparently prevails than in the United States. The country has a long tradition of state intervention in the economy. Credit controls in favor of housing are bolstered by controls over virtually all alternative channels through which domestic credit may flow, as well as by various tax and subsidy and investment-fund devices. Commercial and savings banks and private insurance companies are required to buy mortgage bonds and government bonds to meet specified minimum ratios, and the investment policies of the insurance companies are subject to government guidance in further ways. The national pension fund is the country's dominant nonbank financial intermediary, receiving all obligatory pension contributions made by employers. The Riksbank controls new issues of bonds. It customarily holds 60 to 90 percent of Treasury bills outstanding, and only banks participate in the bill market.[70]

Despite the success sometimes claimed for this system, Swedish academic economists generally oppose its continuation. They mention the difficulty of finding criteria for the nonprice rationing of credit, as well as the rise of queues and gray markets. They favor

---

[67] Hodgman, *Western Europe*, p. 50. It is not clear, of course, that actually achieving a pattern of resource allocation different from what the free-market pattern would have been is an unambiguous criterion of success.

[68] O'Brien, "Central Banking across the Atlantic," p. 9.

[69] Jaffee, "Housing Finance," p. 113.

[70] Hodgman, *Western Europe*, pp. 42-43, 52, 66, and Lindbeck, "Experiments in Sweden," in FRBB, *Techniques*, p. 212 and *passim*.

a shift toward flexible exchange rates and domestic interest rates, control over the money supply, and the use of taxes and subsidies instead of credit controls to influence resource allocation.[71]

What Lessons Can Be Drawn? Allusions to Swedish experience seem typical of a literature that does not so much muster evidence as, rather, diffuse an *impression* of success in foreign countries. Actually, it proves nothing to refer airily, as Senator William Proxmire has done,[72] to the fact that many foreign countries have credit-allocation programs more extensive and far-reaching than the piecemeal policies so far pursued in the United States.[73] Convincing evidence does not emerge from "a casual review of data covering a handful of years in a single country whose continuing housing shortage is among the worst in the world (Sweden)," ignoring the long and "unremittingly dismal" record of "U.S. experience with detailed intervention in capital markets under the Federal Reserve System." [74]

To count as solid evidence, references to foreign success would have to spell out just what was done, and how, and what the results were, including long-run as well as short-run and indirect as well as obvious results, and would have to show why those results are desirable.

In considering what lessons European experience might hold for the United States, we must keep in mind differences between economic conditions and policy objectives there and here. Relevant differences concern the degree of concentration and cartelization in banking, the general competitiveness of the economy, the extent of variety in financial institutions and markets, the degree of official domination of money and capital markets and control over international transactions, the spirit of cooperation between central and

---

71 Hodgman, *Western Europe*, p. 52.

72 "The Federal Reserve is the only major central bank in the world which has refused to assume a responsibility for allocating credit to socially important sectors of the economy. . . . It is high time we brought the Federal Reserve Board into the 20th century." Quoted in O'Brien, "Central Banking across the Atlantic," p. 3.

73 Compare Hodgman, *Western Europe*, pp. 6-7, criticizing two studies published by the House Committee on Banking and Currency.

A study by Lester Thurow and associates, reprinted in U.S., Congress, *Hearings*, pp. 370-76, for example, gives sketchy *descriptions* of foreign credit-allocation measures; it tells, for example, how the Bank of Japan influences credit allocation; but it does not really get into the question of results.

74 Kane, "Discussion," in FRBB, *Policies*, p. 190. Kane is referring to Thurow's paper in the same volume.

commercial bankers, the degree of consensus on national priorities, and the general acceptability of extensive state economic intervention. Despite a context more favorable to use of selective credit controls, dissatisfaction with them in several European countries in recent years has motivated a trend away from them and toward greater reliance, for macroeconomic purposes, on general monetary and budgetary measures. To say the least, European experience has not discredited the standard analysis of circumvention of controls and of the proliferation of controls in attempts to thwart circumvention.[75]

---

[75] Hodgman, *Western Europe*, pp. 1-2, 72, and O'Brien, "Central Banking across the Atlantic," p. 11.

3

WHAT KIND OF ECONOMIC SYSTEM?

A system of selective credit controls is unlikely to achieve its avowed purposes; yet attempts to make it work will impose costs. These include costs of enforcement, compliance, and paperwork.

Financial institutions subject to credit allocations are put at a disadvantage in competing for loanable funds. New institutions and practices emerge to get around the controls. Institutional instability hastens the obsolescence of existing knowledge; so investors, managers, customers, and others must spend time and resources becoming acquainted with new institutions and practices. Regulators and legislators incur costs as they strive to keep abreast of and to plug loopholes. Institutional instability makes it more difficult for the authorities to achieve stability or stable growth of the money supply, even if that were their aim.[1]

Ultimate Consequences

The broadest type of cost is a gradual change in the very nature of the economic system. Selective credit controls undercut "the well functioning and competitive capital markets that exist as a rule in the U.S. today." Unfortunately, as Dwight Jaffee continues, these consequences "are not quickly and easily perceived, since the controls are enacted slowly over time and the markets will appear to adjust to them." Reversing their unhealthy cumulative impact will prove difficult, since institutions that have succeeded in adapting will resist change. The approach of proceeding pragmatically, extending the range of controls as appears necessary, does "not

---

[1] See Thomas Mayer, "The Case against Credit Allocations," *National Review*, December 19, 1975, p. 1491.

look far enough ahead to see that extending selective credit controls over the full set of financial markets will, ultimately, cause the breakdown in the full set." [2]

Undercutting the credit and capital markets weakens existing economic and social institutions and takes a long step toward a centrally "planned" economy. It is hard to suppress a suspicion that this is what some advocates of credit controls desire.

Besides having economic costs, both specific and broad ones, credit-allocation policies are also likely to impose "a political cost. Selective credit policies, by their nature, impinge upon an individual's freedom of choice. In a democratic society such as ours, this must *in and of itself* be judged as a burden of such policies." [3]

Alternatives

Alternatives to selective credit controls are available. One is deregulation. Removing interest-rate ceilings, the ban on demand-deposit interest, and other perversely working regulations would reduce the supposed discriminatory effects of tight money.[4] So would greater steadiness in monetary policy than has so far been achieved —or sought.

On the assumption—still to be examined—that it is desirable to twist patterns of resource allocation and production and consumption away from what would emerge on a free market, the gov-

---

[2] Dwight M. Jaffee, "Housing Finance and Mortgage Market Policy," in Karl Brunner et al., *Government Credit Allocation* (San Francisco: Institute for Contemporary Studies, 1975), pp. 111, 120-21. Jaffee maintains that European experience confirms his appraisal. See also Tommaso Padoa-Schioppa, "Selective Credit Policy: Italy's Recent Experience," Banca Nazionale del Lavoro *Quarterly Review*, no. 112 (March 1975), pp. 50-51.

[3] Ira Kaminow and James M. O'Brien, "Issues in Selective Credit Policies: An Evaluative Essay," in *Studies in Selective Credit Policies*, ed. Ira Kaminow and James M. O'Brien (Philadelphia: Federal Reserve Bank of Philadelphia, 1975), p. 31.

[4] Carl H. Stem makes a broadly similar case for decontrol as a partial remedy for the supposed problems caused by the Eurodollar market, whose evolution in the first place came largely as a response to banking controls in the United States, Britain, and other countries. In this respect the Eurodollar market illustrates one of the main themes of the present study—the ease of evasion of controls, as through institutional innovation. See Stem, "Some Eurocurrency Problems: Credit Expansion, the Regulatory Framework, Liquidity, and Petrodollars," in *Eurocurrencies and the International Monetary System*, ed. Stem et al. (Washington, D.C.: American Enterprise Institute for Public Policy Research, 1976), pp. 283-332, and also Fischer Black's commentary, pp. 336-37.

ernment might well replace inaccurately focused implicit taxes and subsidies with explicit ones. After all, asset reserve requirements and offsets, portfolio ceilings and floors, differential rediscounting privileges, and the like all represent implicit subsidies or taxes placed on governmentally favored or disfavored loans and investments of financial institutions. More broadly, compelling a lending institution to act in what its management would consider a relatively unprofitable way works like a tax on its officially disfavored activities. A more straightforward program would induce lenders to grant favored loans by paying them money raised from taxes on disfavored types.[5] A still more straightforward approach would impinge not on the financing but on the activities themselves (housing or whatever): favored activities could receive subsidies out of revenues raised from taxes on sectors of the economy from which the government wanted to divert resources. Nothing closely analogous to the fungibility of money and credit would then come into play. It seems more promising to aim directly at desired effects on the allocation of real resources than to hope for those effects as a byproduct of tinkering with the financing thought to be linked (and linked loosely, at best) with the activities to be affected.

Where to Apply Corrective Measures

A general principle of welfare economics, furthermore, calls for applying corrective measures at the point of distortion. Applied elsewhere, a supposed corrective measure, instead of exactly offsetting the original distortion, forms a new one that may well do more harm than good on balance.[6] If the free-market pattern of *outputs* of goods and services diverges from some ideal, then corrective measures should apply to outputs. If the market for labor or some

---

[5] Similarly, the American Bankers Association has proposed a tax credit to stimulate investment in a few national-priority areas. A tax credit on income from home mortgages, for example, would encourage such loans. A tax-incentive approach, applied uniformly to all lenders and adapted flexibly to changing conditions, would eliminate the need for an extensive bureaucracy. If the tax credit turned out not to channel funds as desired, then the ABA would support direct subsidies to high-priority borrowers. Beryl F. Sprinkel in U.S., Congress, *Hearings*, p. 158.

[6] See Harry G. Johnson, "Optimal Trade Intervention in the Presence of Domestic Distortions," in Robert E. Baldwin et al., *Trade, Growth, and the Balance of Payments* (Chicago: Rand McNally, 1965), pp. 3-34. Sources or types of "distortion" may include externalities (as explained beginning on page 27 above), controls, and impediments to competition.

other factor of production is somehow distorted, then that is where a corrective measure ideally belongs. If the credit market is distorted, then it is the proper focus for corrective measures. Even so, the most suitable measures may well be taxes and subsidies on borrowing and lending rather than direct credit controls.

More needs to be said about the consequences of a supposed corrective measure applied at the wrong point. Suppose that the government imposes controls in the credit markets in hopes of remedying distortions actually centered elsewhere and that these controls do succeed in making credit cheaper or more readily available in some sectors of the economy at the expense of other sectors. Changes in outputs of particular goods and services will not be the only results; methods of financing and methods of production will also respond to the changed credit terms. Cheapened credit will give the favored firms an incentive to finance themselves more heavily by debt and less heavily by equity capital (from selling stock and plowing back profits) than they would otherwise do, and there is no obvious reason why such a shift from equity to debt financing is socially desirable. It can be undesirable if the greater use of debt causes more insolvencies and bankruptcies and thus more instability and social disorganization in business downturns.

Furthermore, a cheapening of credit or capital leads firms to adopt more highly capital-intensive productive processes than they otherwise would.[7] Inputs are to some extent substitutable for each other in production processes, and the mix that a firm adopts depends in part on the prices it must pay. Artificially favorable credit terms induce firms to use capital more lavishly than is warranted by scarcity and productivity throughout the economy as a whole,[8] while firms disadvantaged by the credit controls tend to substitute other factors of production for capital, using those others more lavishly than their scarcities and productivities warrant. Excess employments of capital in some firms and of other factors in other firms, instead of just neutralizing each other (let alone improving on the operation of unrigged markets), constitute economic waste.

For an analogy, consider what would happen if the government subsidized the employment of labor in some sectors of the economy and taxed its employment in other sectors. Or, for a still closer

---

[7] Rudolph G. Penner, "Taxation and the Allocation of Credit," in *Studies*, ed. Kaminow and O'Brien, p. 93, and Mayer, "The Case against Credit Allocations," p. 1472.

[8] Kenneth Lyon, *Some of the Economic Effects of Subsidizing Rural Electrification* (Ph.D. diss., University of Chicago, 1970).

analogy to administrative credit controls, suppose that the government restricts the employment of labor in some sectors so that other sectors will have artificially cheap and abundant labor. Unless these measures happen to serve as correctives for distortions centered specifically in the labor markets, they themselves violate criteria of efficient resource allocation. Some sectors will employ too little labor in conjunction with other factors of production, while other sectors employ too much. Waste of factors other than labor in the former sectors does not offset waste of labor in the latter sectors; the different wastes add up instead of canceling each other. The same general principle applies if capital, rather than labor, is the productive factor subject to administrative allocation: factors become used in inefficient combinations.

For believers in the democratic process, applying corrective taxes and subsidies to economic distortions has a further advantage over credit controls: it is relatively explicit and clear and improves the chances that citizens can monitor what their government is doing. Democracy works less well when the government operates indirectly, concealing who loses and who gains from its measures. Whether explicit policies, though healthy from a democratic point of view, are realistic from the personal viewpoint of politicians is another question.

In listing alternatives to selective credit controls, we should again mention, for completeness, the establishment of special financial institutions (such as those named on page 6 above) to aid governmentally favored sectors of the economy.

Should the Government Guide the Pattern of Economic Activity?

Until now we have left the idea unchallenged that the government ought, somehow, to make the pattern of economic activity different from what would emerge in a free market, and that it should do so beyond merely supplying public goods (defense and the like) and charging for them through taxation. We have simply been considering arguments for and methods of this further intervention. We have been considering whether—in view of possibilities of circumvention and of other difficulties—credit controls are the most suitable measures. After all, the government cannot actually determine the national pattern of production and consumption, let alone achieve for individuals their ultimate goals in life. Even with this economic pattern, all it can do is establish and tinker with rules and constraints on people's activities and transactions in the hope that the result will be more satisfactory—by some criterion or other—than the pattern hitherto observed.[9]

Proximate objectives of economic policy are relatively specific, such as desired influences on patterns of credit and resource allocation, production, and consumption. Ultimate objectives include high real income, stability, equity, and so forth, and beyond them, the still more ultimate objective of a good society in which individuals are free to pursue their own happiness and can cooperate effectively in doing so. As Kaminow and O'Brien rightly imply, "the current method of relating ultimate goals to proximate objectives" proceeds backwards. It focuses on a particular good and asks what social goals the government might advance by encouraging (or discouraging) its production. A more logical approach would start "with the ultimate goal and [ask] what composition of output is best suited to achieving these goals."[10] The current political approach, in other words, is to propose controls and then think up reasons for desiring their supposed consequences. It would be more logical to test proposals against a conception of the good society.

The burden of arguing that specified influences on the pattern of economic activity are desirable ought to rest on the advocates of controls. After all, there is a presumption against proliferating government economic interventions lest they undermine a free-market economy, democratic government, and a free society generally. The advocates of credit controls have not made a persuasive case. They have many strings to their bow, but each of them is weak. Some of their arguments are formally valid—they are not logical or economic nonsense—yet their applicability to the real world is doubtful.

It is all too easy to make a list of goods, activities, or economic sectors that would superficially seem to deserve special favor. It is all too easy to enlist abstract theoretical arguments in their behalf. Yet steering productive resources into favored activities means withholding them from others, and no one knows just which of all other activities will be disadvantaged most. How can one be sure that those shrunken activities are not themselves especially meritorious in terms of the standard arguments? Political decisions on economic affairs, as the nineteenth century economist Frederic Bastiat used to

---

[9] See Rutledge Vining, "On Two Foundation Concepts of the Theory of Political Economy," *Journal of Political Economy*, vol. 77 (March/April 1969), pp. 199-218.

[10] Kaminow and O'Brien, "Issues," p. 29. One might object, though, on the grounds developed in the article cited in the preceding footnote and alluded to in the accompanying text here, to the very notion of a most suitable "composition of output."

argue, suffer from overemphasis on the *seen* to the relative neglect of the *unseen*: desired and relatively obvious results get too much attention relative to unrecognized repercussions, some of which may occur in remote sectors of the economic system and only after long time lags.

A not-quite-explicit distinction is sometimes made between relatively essential goods or activities, on the one hand, and relatively frivolous or superficial ones, on the other hand,[11] with the implication that the former have greater beneficial externalities or merit quality than the latter. Goods or activities are sometimes classified as essential or frivolous according to whether they contribute to production or merely to "unnecessary" consumption. Such distinctions are dubious. All production supposedly aims at satisfying human wants, immediately or ultimately. Constructing machines or factories or houses is not inherently more worthy than producing restaurant meals or nightclub entertainment, for the machines or factories or houses are pointless unless they sooner or later give rise to goods or service that do satisfy human wants. To favor production-oriented over consumption-oriented activities is to prefer a roundabout pursuit of ultimate consumer satisfactions to their more direct achievement merely because of greater roundaboutness; it is to confuse ends and means.

Barring specific known distortions for which controls or taxes and subsidies might be a corrective, the idea naturally arises of letting ultimate consumers appraise "essentiality." Give up trying to make sweeping philosophical comparisons; instead, let people act on their own comparisons of the satisfactions expected from another dollar's worth of this and another dollar's worth of that. Let consumers and businessmen judge and act on the intensities of the wants that various goods can satisfy, either directly or by contributing to further processes of production. Let them bid for the goods they want and for the productive resources, including capital or credit, used in producing them.

By now we are familiar with the standard theoretical reservations about this suggestion. Yet how can one be confident that supposed externalities are genuine and important, that supposed merit wants really deserve cultivation, or that favoring particular goods really will accomplish a desired income redistribution?[12] Any one of a great many goods, considered by itself, might seem deserving

---

11 Jacques H. David, "Discussion," in FRBB, *Techniques*, p. 162, mentions the role of such distinctions in French credit policy.

12 Kenneth Clarkson, *Food Stamps and Nutrition* (Washington, D.C.: American Enterprise Institute for Public Policy Research, 1975).

of special favor; yet the *relative* deservingness of different goods may remain highly uncertain, particularly when no one knows just how sharply the diversion of resources into particular lines of production will impair production in other meritorious lines.

Furthermore, particular goods do not possess qualities deserving of special consideration globally, or by their very nature. On the contrary, usefulness or desirability is a relation between things and human wants; and the marginal usefulness or desirability of a particular thing is the smaller the more abundant the thing is. Ideally, decisions about restricting or promoting the production of various things ought to consider their usefulness *at the margin.* It is easy to imagine circumstances in which an additional dollar's worth or an additional ounce of penicillin or polio vaccine would contribute less to human satisfaction than an additional dollar's worth or an additional ounce of orchids. Yet a program of government *priorities* can hardly take account of how relatively desirable different things are *at the margin.*

Let us reconsider the idea of using credit controls to help redistribute income or wealth from rich to poor people, and let us set aside the question whether compulsory redistribution is the proper business of government. Tinkering with credit is an indirect and imprecise way of seeking the desired result. Instead of working straightforwardly, it steers credit away from rich borrowers or from the financing of goods and services heavily consumed by rich people toward poor borrowers or toward the production of goods and services heavily consumed by poor people. This, rather, is what credit allocation would do if it worked in the best conceivable way. Actually, steering credit toward housing, for example, in effect subsidizes consumers of housing in general, and not just poor ones. It might well work perversely, mainly benefiting middle-income and wealthy home buyers, building contractors, highly paid craftsmen, and firms supplying materials to the construction industry. As a way of helping poor people, it is costly in relation to its effectiveness. Giving them money would be a more precise way.

Even if the authorities did decide to steer credit toward housing for the sake of income redistribution or externalities or for some other reason, numerous detailed decisions would remain to be made. What kind of housing should be financed? Would it be single-family homes, multifamily homes, or apartment buildings? Would it be urban or suburban or rural housing? Would vacation homes as well as first homes be eligible? How would special favor be allocated between high- and low-cost housing and between renovation and new construction? Would buyers of raw land, developers, and construction companies obtain direct benefits under the program, or only ultimate home buyers? Which particular business firms, if any, would be subject to favorable or adverse credit allocations? [13]

A credit-allocation program would be hard put to allow for regional differences. Mortgage credit might be amply available in some regions with a low demand for housing while the national market was generally pinched. A blanket policy of forcing credit into housing could well be inefficient and counterproductive in some areas.[14] Again the problems of centrally mobilizing knowledge come to mind.

It is difficult, furthermore, to categorize credit as serving a particular purpose. Suppose that a bank makes a loan to a firm that leases dump trucks to building contractors. Such financing is vital to construction, yet it would not count as a housing loan.[15] For a further example, consider a businessman who wants to add a wing to his store and, incidentally, hire a dozen more people. A credit-allocation program would probably assign lower priority to his loan than to a loan for low-income housing, even though the prospective tenants of the housing project might want the jobs he could create. Suppose a steel corporation wants to build up its inventory of coal in readiness for a strike. Such foresight might well spare the national economy significant dislocation; yet what would probably be deemed "excess inventory accumulation" would fare poorly under a credit-allocation program. The controllers could not meaningfully distinguish between essential and nonessential activities because such a distinction defies human wisdom in a society as complex as ours.[16]

For reasons like these and for reasons concerning how the political process works, and also in view of ample experience with controls, it is unrealistic to expect the government to choose "social priorities" reasonably. Consider, for example, the botch of energy policy, including the long record of subsidizing energy consumption in travel and transport by automobile, truck, and airplane (through the underpricing of road and airport facilities),[17] and also including

---

13 Eli Shapiro in FRBB, *Policies*, p. 202, in a "Discussion" of Lester Thurow's proposal for asset reserve requirements.

14 Beryl F. Sprinkel in U.S., Congress, *Hearings*, p. 25.

15 Carter H. Golembe Associates, Inc., *Commercial Banks and National Housing Policy* (Chicago: Association of Reserve City Bankers, 1971), p. 25.

16 Treasury Secretary Simon in U.S., Congress, *Hearings*, pp. 19-20.

17 Ross Eckert, *Airports and Congestion: A Problem of Misplaced Subsidies* (Washington, D.C.: American Enterprise Institute for Public Policy Research, 1972).

the continued grant of tax exemptions and subsidized loans to rural electric cooperatives, even while government officials plead for energy conservation. In view of such performances, what reason is there to expect that all relevant considerations will be taken into account and duly weighed against each other in the assignment of credit priorities? (The concept of priorities, we should remember, is itself a mistake, since it is a global concept, whereas relevant choices take place at the margin). Arguments for promoting occupant-ownership of housing are well known, for example; yet there are also reasonable arguments against it, which, however, are almost always neglected in political discussions. After all, the government is no philosopher-king, acting benevolently and coherently with a single superior mind.[18] On the contrary, the government is a congeries of individual persons—politicians, legislators, executives, bureaucrats, judges—each operating with his own particular motivations and opportunities, and many often operating at cross-purposes with one another.

This is the lesson that Representative Henry Reuss should have drawn from his examples of alleged credit allocation by the Federal Reserve for purposes that turned out, with hindsight, to be unwise.[19] Reuss's point was that if the Federal Reserve can allocate credit in unwise ways, it could just as well allocate credit wisely, provided only that Congress instructed it to do so. Actually, there is little reason to doubt the Federal Reserve's good intentions and little reason to suppose that reciting good intentions in an act of Congress would make them work out better in the future.

Why Is the Idea So Durable?

If the case for selective credit controls is as weak and the case against them as strong as those cases seem to be, why is the idea of such controls nevertheless so durable? First, the idea of steering credit toward worthy activities seems practical, down-to-earth, and realistic; unlike ivory-tower admiration of the free market, it deals with nuts and bolts. It fits in well with certain prevalent traits of thinking. It seems to have become a widely accepted axiom nowadays that it is the job of government to promote all good things and suppress all bad things and to heed all complaints about the

[18] For an example of tacitly regarding the government (mislabeled "society") as such a philosopher-king, see Thurow, "Proposals," in FRBB, *Policies*, esp. pp. 183-84.

[19] U.S., Congress, *Hearings*, p. 209. See also p. 10 above.

shortcomings of reality, including supposed "imperfections" of the market.[20]

Many persons are no doubt sincerely persuaded by the standard theoretical arguments for government intervention. By calling for *action*—government action—to promote worthy and deter less worthy activities, some people can enjoy a feeling of being pragmatic and progressive and of being on the side of the angels.[21] By introducing and supporting bills to that effect, legislators can seek to demonstrate to themselves and their constituents that they are alert to problems and that they "care." By introducing bills and holding hearings, they can cultivate reputations for expertise in particular fields. Legislators, as well as outside experts, can display originality—of a rather routine sort—by thinking up new measures to promote good and deter bad activities. It is not even necessary to spell out the specifics clearly. A politician can gain esteem even by sponsoring legislation that, instead of providing a solution to a supposed problem, simply calls for a solution, passing the buck to the President or some federal agency to fill in the details.[22] By en-

---

[20] Acceptance of this axiom is akin to an attitude described by Ortega y Gasset. Ortega's *mass-man* tends to take the wonders of modern industrial society for granted. He regards them practically as ultimate facts of nature, which simply exist. He forgets about the genius, dreams, work, saving, sacrifice, boldness, and devotion necessary to develop and maintain our material civilization. Nobody deserves credit for its wonders. But he holds their suppliers blameworthy if they do not measure up to his growing expectations. And he regards the government as his tool for getting him what he wants. (Ortega's concept of mass-man is not a sneer at members of particular social classes or poor or relatively ungifted people. Mass-men, as Ortega defines them, are characterized not by their incomes, wealth, or talents but by their attitudes; they are found even in the highest social classes.) See José Ortega y Gasset, *The Revolt of the Masses* (New York: Norton, 1957; original Spanish edition, 1930).

[21] One suspects that some such feeling goes far toward explaining why many successful businessmen join in the clamor for government economic planning of one kind or another: they have already made their mark in the business world and are searching for new satisfactions and new ways to achieve distinction.

As Alan A. Walters has suggested, influence over government decisions "often supplies the emotional needs of humanitarians and others who feel they must frequently demonstrate their compassion and their moral superiority." "The Politicization of Economic Decisions," *The Banker*, October 1975, Reprint Paper 1 (Los Angeles: International Institute for Economic Research, 1976), p. 9.

[22] On the empty, symbolic character of many ostensible solutions to supposed problems, see Amitai Etzioni, "The Grand Shaman," *Psychology Today*, vol. 6 (November 1972), pp. 88-92, 142-43. Theodore J. Lowi, similarly, has emphasized

acting new powers and responsibilities for the Federal Reserve in the field of credit allocation, for example, congressmen can feel that they are "doing something" about supposed problems. If things do not work out right, they have a strengthened basis for criticizing the Federal Reserve. They can complain, in effect: We gave you good instructions and good tools, and still you did wrong.

"Scientism," as F. A. Hayek calls it,[23] is another trait of thinking that contributes to support for government intervention. A full definition would be out of place here, but one aspect of scientism is the feeling that results somehow do not count unless they have been consciously planned for and deliberately contrived. The scientistic attitude runs in parallel with ignorance of the coordinating and self-adjusting properties of a market economy and of the information-transmitting as well as incentive function of prices. Someone harboring the scientistic attitude does not understand how millions of persons and companies, trading freely among themselves, can express the relative urgency of their wants and provide for the satisfaction of the ones they consider most urgent. He believes, instead, that a grandmotherly state must take charge; and he performs feats of routine originality in thinking of new ways in which it might do so.

Scientism no doubt ties in with the idea sometimes met that selective credit controls can be useful for macroeconomic stabilization purposes. How prudent management of the total money supply might prevent inflation is not obvious to everyone. What seems more obvious, though, than to check total spending by restricting the credit that would fuel particular expenditures? The idea is sometimes encountered, also, that selective credit controls are an alternative to high interest rates, which, it is feared, would depress bond and stock prices, victimize poor people, and work other evils.

The phenomenon of spurious consensus probably works to the advantage of credit-control proposals. Each of us might be in favor of high-social-priority activities; but our apparent consensus is

the irresponsibility of enacting laws that vaguely express good intentions while leaving implementation and interpretation up to executive agencies and the courts. Such irresponsibility tends to cause deterioration of the legal and political systems. Laws calling for steering credit toward supposedly worthy and away from supposedly unworthy uses would seem to be a prime example of the sort of irresponsible legislative vagueness that Lowi criticizes. See his *The End of Liberalism* (New York: Norton, 1969) and *The Politics of Disorder* (New York: Basic Books, 1971).

[23] "Scientism and the Study of Society," *Economica*, 1942-1944, reprinted in *The Counter-Revolution of Science* (Glencoe: Free Press, 1952), part 1.

spurious if we differ in our conceptions of priorities, of what measures are to be employed to serve them, and of what side effects those measures might have. Tunnel vision can contribute to spurious consensus: People can see how the favored activities will supposedly benefit from the controls, yet not recognize the diffuse harm imposed on other activities. "Given the fact that every single form of credit not now controlled has had support as a 'priority item' from some segment of society," Ezra Solomon offers the following conjecture: "If the question of just *how* direct credit controls should be applied is answered first, the support for the idea of using direct controls at all will fall at least one-half."[24]

Using credit controls to favor particular activities or members of particular sectors of the economic system hides the costs of doing so. If they work, credit controls have the effect of subsidizing favored activities from the proceeds of taxes on others. Since those taxes are hidden, the use of credit controls provides a way of serving special interests under the rhetoric of serving the general interest.[25] It is a way of concealing—even from the politicians themselves—the costs of granting special favors.

Referring in particular to the distributional arguments for selective credit controls, Edward J. Kane characterizes congressional shifting of responsibility to the Federal Reserve as "a cynical political gambit designed to buy time and reelection without having to confront the searing political problems of our time. The Fed cannot itself make the hard choices necessary to effect sizeable changes in the distribution of income and opportunity." It can only serve as scapegoat for particular congressmen and the lobbies that influence their decisions. Congressmen want to tell their constituents that *something* is being done, while the lobbies want to block any real change. The Federal Reserve's past failures in administering selec-

---

[24] "Monetary Policy and Credit Allocation—The Basic Issues," in FRBB, *Techniques*, p. 13.

[25] The following section from a resolution adopted by the convention of the National Farmers Union in March 1974 is a particularly clear example of self-seeking by special interests: "Enact a national usury statute, with an 8-percent ceiling on interest rates. The statute should provide for allocation by the federal government of credit among users in the event of scarce supply, with highest priority to farmers and ranchers for agricultural purposes. . . ." (Reproduced in U.S., Congress, *Hearings*, p. 155.) Another recent example is the proposal by a number of Northeastern state governors that a regional energy and development corporation be created. The corporation would obtain capital from the state governments and would float bonds backed by federal guarantees. Felix Rohatyn, "Reviving the Northeast," *Washington Post*, April 17, 1977, p. C8.

tive controls make it "a candidate that can meet both objectives, combining the appearance of action with little probability of success."[26]

As already suggested, several probable reasons for the respectability of the idea of selective credit controls indicate abuse of the democratic process. Doing things indirectly, stressing who gains and hiding who loses from government programs, using the income-distribution argument in a demagogic way—all are examples. Enactment of selective controls would be a prime example of over-burdening the democratic process, for effective economic planning cannot be accomplished democratically.

An Appraisal in Context

Credit-control proposals should be appraised as manifestations of a way of thinking and as an approach to policy. They are examples of favoring government economic planning over the market economy. They exemplify casual attitudes such as scientism and such as the mass-man's assumption that the material wonders of modern civilization exist spontaneously and that it is the government's job to fix up "imperfections" to suit him.[27]

The issue of selective credit controls falls under the broader question of whether policy should serve principle or expediency, the latter meaning to act on the supposed merits of each individual case, narrowly considered. In relation to the whole wide range of government economic policies, the question of credit allocation *is* an individual case. The benefits and especially the costs of any such particular measure are hard to fathom. This and other reasons argue for framing policy with prime attention not to the supposed merits of each narrow case but rather to the general framework of rules within which persons and companies can pursue their own goals. (In philosophical terminology, the argument favors rules-utilitarianism over act-utilitarianism.)

If identifying credit-control proposals for what they are—one strand in a comprehensive policy stance—means taking an ideological position, so be it. We should not flinch from identifying and confronting ideologies, which means confronting alternative pictures of a good society. Do we really want government activism to proceed so far that the government tries to determine and enforce priorities regarding the financing and production of all sorts of

[26] Edward J. Kane, "Discussion," in FRBB, *Policies*, p. 198.
[27] Recall footnote 20, this chapter.

goods and services (and not just of public goods)? Do we really want to recommend more government activism as a solution even to problems largely rooted in existing government activism? (Recall how controls over interest rates, for example, have created some of the distortions that give rise to calls for governmental remedies.) Do we want to invite abuses by making control over the government a more valuable prize than existing governmental activism already makes it?

Selective credit controls are even open to objection on ethical grounds. To describe the issue as one of private versus governmental credit allocation [28] is to accord equal respect to people's use of their own earnings and forcible interference with that use. That view accords the government as much right to impose an allocation or reallocation as people have to lend or invest their own money as they see fit (and as financial institutions have in lending or investing money entrusted to them). That view sets aside the question of who has a right to do what in favor of the question of which expected pattern of credit and resource allocation appeals more to politicians and other outside observers.

Government credit allocation would contribute to a proliferation of government activities so vast that the people's elected representatives, let alone the people themselves, could not monitor them. It would widen the scope for lawsuits and for court decisions creating unforeseen legal precedents. Greater government involvement in the economy would further undermine possibilities of democratic control over government itself.

---

[28] Recall chapter 1, under "Imperfect Markets and Discrimination."

Cover and book design: Pat Taylor